T0158940

Marriage

What's That?

Glenda Kyle

WESTBOW
PRESS®
A DIVISION OF THOMAS NELSON
& ZONDERVAN

All scriptures are taken from the KING JAMES VERSION (KJV): KING JAMES VERSION, public domain.

Interior images by Lauri Berka

WestBow Press books may be ordered through booksellers or by contacting:

WestBow Press
A Division of Thomas Nelson & Zondervan
1663 Liberty Drive
Bloomington, IN 47403
www.westbowpress.com
1 (866) 928-1240

ISBN: 978-1-5127-7281-4 (sc)
ISBN: 978-1-5127-7283-8 (hc)
ISBN: 978-1-5127-7282-1 (e)

Library of Congress Control Number: 2017900898

Print information available on the last page.

WestBow Press rev. date: 02/17/2017

I thank Almighty God for giving me a husband who honors the marriage covenant and who loves me unconditionally.

May the Most High God richly bless your sacred covenant of marriage. To God be the glory; great things He has done.

Contents

Preface

Upon completion of *My Child, Walk With Me*, I truly believed it was my last book. The Lord had not spoken to me about another one. I came to the conclusion that I was at the end of investing into my grandchildren's lives through books.

A short time ago, I was engaged in a Bible study discussion where everyone was talking about divorce, separation, wedding... As a joke, I simply offered premarital counseling for our associate pastor and her fiancée– some free advice. It was just a humorous comment.

My husband, Kirby, and I have instructed couples on communication for eight years, taught marriage classes in our church on multiple occasions, and have counseled our children and their friends before their appointed date. We have come from a lineage of long marriages (fifty plus years on both sides of our families), and Kirby and I celebrated our forty eighth wedding anniversary this year. I thought we were pretty qualified.

From this simple humorous question, "Would you like some premarital counseling?", came one member in our class speaking up. "That's going to be your next book." Then another one chimed in, "Yea, you're right. That is going to be your next book." At this point, I'm in shock! It was only a jovial comment volunteering to counsel two people, not write for a year on the subject of marriage.

Driving home that night from Bible study, I pondered what had been said. Finally, I decided to ask God what He thought. My question to Him was, "Okay Lord, if I'm to write another book, what would You call it?" God likes questions. His immediate reply was *Marriage – What's That?* Having been stopped at a traffic light, I threw up my hands and declared, "Well, I guess I'm writing another book."

The next day I'm still pondering all that had taken place the night before. I'm sitting on my back porch swing where the Lord and I often visit (my secret place). I asked Him another question. "Why me?" You see, I see myself as just an ordinary person that's not well known. I'm not in the public eye like some great prestigious women that I know. God answered me with, "You have a lot to give." To be honest, my next thought wasn't the best. I told the Lord that I was glad He thought I had a lot to give. However, I questioned whether I had enough knowledge, wisdom, or insight to write a book on marriage. I let Him know He was going to have to tell people about *Marriage – What's That?* as if He had planned on keeping it a secret.

I don't pretend to have all the answers on marriage, and Kirby and I still are growing in some areas of our own marriage. I do know that I've been given an assignment. Because I want to do my *best* for the Lord, I'll share the *best* that I can.

Since our oldest granddaughter is marrying age, this book is definitely timely. I see *Marriage – What's That?* as being a handbook on how marriage should look.

It's important for you to know up front that I'm not trying to be your marriage counselor. I'm not trying to fix broken marriages. What you receive from this book is up to you. It's your choice. I will say that God restores willing hearts.

I want couples to see God's heart for marriage. Couples need to see marriage as unique, special, and precious. Marriages should be healthy, strong, and lasting. We should want to return to the garden of Eden where peace abounds. We should want to walk and talk with God like Adam and Eve did in the coolness of the day. Your heavenly Father wants to minister direction and purpose, provision and promotion, restoration and healing, affirmation and love, identity, wisdom, and comfort in marriages.

Ultimately, this book should be a picture of a happy and fulfilled marriage. Be abundantly blessed as you walk out the most holy institution on earth – *Marriage*.

What Is God's Plan for Marriage?

As I pondered on how to format this book on marriage, it occurred to me that since God called it *Marriage – What's That?*, it should be formatted as questions. So I started my quest by thinking of questions that would touch every area of a healthy marriage. My first question is probably the most important one of all: In the beginning, what was God's plan for marriage?

Many individuals would probably like to get right into the relationship of marriage instead of looking at God's plan. However, looking at God's plan first helps us see the *best* picture for a healthy marriage.

God's plan was perfect. It consisted of His creation, Adam, who had everything at his fingertips, lacking nothing. God blessed every living thing to be fruitful, to multiply, and to replenish the earth. Adam was given the authority to dominate or rule over the fish of the sea, the fowl of the air, and everything that moved over the earth (Genesis 1:28). God placed Adam in the garden of Eden to "dress it, and keep it" (Genesis 2:15).

God made man to be His highest creation, made in God's image, to procreate and expand the garden of Eden over the entire world. The garden was a place of peace, rest, health, prosperity, and life. It consisted of all things good. Nothing was missing, and nothing was broken; lack and death didn't exist. "God saw that it was good" (Genesis 1:25).

As Adam named all of the animals, he realized there were none like him. God is a God of relationship. He didn't want Adam to be lonely, so He created Eve from Adam's rib to be his companion, someone to walk along beside him. She was to be his helpmate, someone that would back his plans, help him fulfill his purpose, and be an encourager and supporter as they went through the day. She was to love him unconditionally with no strings attached. She was to be *tenderly devoted* to Adam.

God set up headship. Man is subject to God, and the woman is subject to her husband (1 Corinthians 11:3).

The garden of Eden had everything that Adam and Eve required. All needs were met: food, water, and even riches (gold, bdellium, and onyx). God made only one request. "But of the tree of the knowledge of good and evil, thou shalt not eat of it..." (Genesis 2:17). When Adam and Eve did eat from this tree, sin entered the garden, and relationship with God was broken.

God so wanted to keep a relationship with His creation. He wanted His creation to learn from Him through spiritual revelation, to communicate, and to fellowship with Him. Eating from the tree of the knowledge of good and evil would allow worldly human reasoning (logic) to enter the world, the I sin: I know best.

God's way is life. Doing things without God is death. After the curse, man began toiling to survive. For the woman, painful child bearing was her lot through life without God.

You know, God loves His creation sooo much. He couldn't let His people die. More than anything else, He wanted to restore relationship back to Himself. To accomplish this, something or someone had to take the punishment for sin. Justice was required. This sacrifice had to be precious, valuable, perfect – a blood sacrifice.

In God's eyes, His only son, Jesus, was the only thing that fit the criteria. God gave the most precious thing He had for you and me. We were bought back at a great price. Jesus took our punishment so relationship with God could be restored. That says much as to how important, special, and highly favored we are to Papa God.

Being in the presence of the Most High God, the everlasting God who is Father of all that is, is the most precious and valuable moment we have. He restores us. It's like stepping back into the garden of Eden.

Is your plan the same plan God has for marriage?

Genesis 1:28   Genesis 2:11–12
Genesis 2:15   1 Corinthians 11:3
Genesis 2:17

What Does God Say about Marriage?

Let's start by discussing God's covenant with His people. Papa God really wanted to provide for His people in all areas of their lives. To accomplish this through the ages, God would make covenants with His people. If His creation would agree (partner with authority), God Almighty (El Shaddai) would provide the power for partnership. You can see many covenants or promises made between God and man throughout scripture. Let's take a look at a few of them.

In Genesis, we see Noah agreeing with God to build the ark. In turn, God makes a covenant with Noah, saying no more would He destroy those on the earth with floods. Papa God gave the rainbow as a sign of His commitment. When the rains were heavy, it was God's way of helping His people remember the covenant He had made with Noah and those on earth.

Later in Genesis, because Abram believes God for a son, the Lord (Adonai) makes a covenant with Abram. God identifies himself to Abram and announces a name change. He would be called Abraham because he was to be the father of many nations. He would produce kings.

God also gives Abraham land for his people and makes him wealthy. God states that Abraham's seed will multiply as many as the stars. God's token between Himself and Abraham is circumcision. Removal of the foreskin from the male is God's reminder that this is a generational covenant. All those who believe in our Lord have the blessing of Abraham for the taking. Many today still circumcise their male infants.

Continuing a little farther, we see Papa God covenanting with Sarai, changing her name to Sarah. I think it's interesting that the *h* from Yahweh (Lord) was breathed into both names to form Abraham and Sarah. Both were beyond child-bearing years when Isaac was conceived. Life was breathed into each to fulfill this covenant, an everlasting covenant for the future generations.

The next covenant is probably the most known in all the world. This one was made between God and Moses and the Jewish people. Because the Israelites wanted to do things their way instead of listening to God and following Him, God had to set up laws for them to follow. That way, they could see their faults and shortcomings – their sins.

These laws were the Ten Commandments written on stone. These tablets signified the token by which the Jewish people would remember His words. Exodus 34:10 states, "Behold I will make a covenant before all thy people. I will do marvels, such as have not been done in all the earth, nor in any nation: and all the people among which thou art shall see the work of the Lord: for it is a terrible [awesome] thing that I will do with thee." We are to remember.

Another part of the covenant with Moses is found in Exodus 25. God instructs Moses on the construction of the Ark of the Covenant that was to hold the tablets – the testimony. Where the ark resided, God's presence (Jahovah-shammah) remained. The people were blessed and peace (Jehovah-shalom) reigned. God's presence (Jehovah-raah, the shepherd) was also manifested as a cloud by day and fire by night for protection and guidance. You could call these visual aids tokens for the children of Israel to remember and honor His presence.

Down the line came the covenant between God and Solomon. God gave Solomon great wisdom while he reigned as the king of the Jewish nation, wisdom far above all others. Because he asked God for understanding to discern judgment instead of a long life, riches, or the lives of his enemies, God gave Solomon phenomenal wisdom and understanding. People would come from afar, having heard of his abilities to understand, discern, and judge his nation. All that Solomon accomplished during his reign was a token of how God blessed Israel.

Exodus 19:5 states, "Now therefore, if ye will obey my voice indeed, and keep my covenant, then ye shall be a peculiar treasure unto me above all people: for all the earth is mine" – a treasure that is His, a treasure that's unusual and special. We become set apart when we keep covenant.

We've taken a brief look at covenants that the Lord has made with some of the major players in the Bible. God is a covenant God. I'm sure that because we're made in the image of God, it was easy for human beings to pick up the practice of making covenants.

In Jewish history, we find Abraham and Abimelech in covenant over a water well. Peace was made, and a feast sealed the agreement. We find Laban and Jacob covenanting for peace over the land. As a token, stones were heaped as a pillar monument, and a feast was enjoyed.

Probably the most remembered covenants between two individuals were the ones made between David and Jonathan (1 Samuel 20:16–17). Because of their great friendship, Jonathan helped to protect David from the wrath of his father, Saul. David and Jonathan were devoted friends. The robe that was given to David was the token of their friendship. Both young men sought peace and safety.

The most important covenant ever made is the covenant between God and His people. God giving His Son as a sacrifice for our sins was the greatest covenant ever made. Jesus laid down His life for you and me. For what? It was for relationship, a free gift for the taking. Here, the token is the Holy Spirit living within us. When we confess and believe, we restore relationship with Papa God. Restoring relationship is number one with our heavenly Father (Jehovah-tsidkenu, the Lord our righteousness).

Today is no different in the covenant world between individuals. We shake hands, draw up contracts, make a promise or vow, or recite an oath. To God, the marriage covenant is the most important covenant between man and woman. Unlike God, I'm not sure most couples even know why or what they're doing at that moment of declaration.

Remember those wedding vows? Kirby and I used traditional vows. Our marriage vows were not original or elegant, but they were recited to each other proclaiming to the world our commitment.

I, _____, take thee _____, to be my lawfully wedded husband/wife, to have and to hold from this day forward, for better or worse, for richer or poorer, in sickness and in health, to love and to cherish as long as we both shall live, so help me God.

Some couples write their own vows to proclaim in front of family and friends solidifying their commitment. During the wedding ceremony, wedding rings are given as a token of the vows and for a remembrance of this special day. Usually after the wedding, there is a feast of some sort to celebrate this spectacular event. Does this sound or look familiar?

As with God, we're to be covenant people. A marriage commitment should not be taken lightly. In God's eyes, it's "for as long as we both shall live." As my mom would say, "There's no ifs, ands, or buts about it." Marriage is a serious commitment and responsibility that requires accountability. It's a vital promise that's to be honored. Consequently, it's imperative that we know our spouse is the right one. Your mate will have an influence in every area of your life to come.

Do you understand the *what and why* of covenant? What covenant will you make for your future?

Genesis 9:15–17

Genesis 17:2–21

Exodus 34:10

Exodus 25

1 Kings 3:11

Exodus 19:5

John 3:16

1 Samuel 20:16–17

John 15:13

Romans 10:9

What Do I Do to Find a Mate?

As I write this question, my mind goes back to when I was eighteen years old and in nursing school. I remember having very little time to reflect upon a mate. Yet, in the back of my mind, I knew what I wanted in a partner for life. I sort of had his looks in mind. I wanted him to be taller than me. The rest was pretty much up for discussion on looks. However, *who he is* was more important. He needed to be trustworthy, hard working, goal oriented, caring, and have a good sense of humor. I remember asking God to send me someone before my graduation date three years out. (The Lord loves to give you the desires of your heart, when you delight in Him.)

My conversation with God consisted of what I wanted in a husband and when I wanted to be married. Beyond this, I went about being the *best* me I could be on a daily basis. I didn't try to find a husband. I believed Papa God, the one who sees and provides (El-Roi and Jehovah- Jireh), would show me whom He had chosen for me.

I met Kirby about a week into my first semester at Texas Eastern School of Nursing. I went home with Kay, one of my classmates, and met Kirby in the town grocery store. My first impressions of him were not the best. He came out from behind the meat market counter wearing a bloody apron and acting like a know-it-all. I saw him arrogant and egotistical, you could say, "full of himself." Kay and I had pierced our ears, and we were looking for small bottles of rubbing alcohol to keep our ears from becoming infected. I will say Kirby was pretty knowledgeable in solving our dilemma of a small bottle.

For Kay to go out with her boyfriend that weekend, she had to find a date for me. You guessed it. After meeting Kirby for about fifteen minutes, he filled that spot. I wouldn't call it a blind date, but it was pretty "dog-gone" close.

Since school was so demanding, my focus was strictly on books. I was finishing a three year program of eighteen to twenty one hours a semester plus working in the hospital. I probably slept an average of four hours a night through the week. Consequently, I tried to make up the sleep deprivation on the weekends.

I still remember when Papa God said Kirby was the one I was to marry. Not only was I surprised he was the one, I realized I really didn't know Kirby that well. I'd had an occasional date with him over the past year but didn't know much more about him than when we first met. He was a very closed person. At this point, I figured I had better get busy. By the end of the second year of school, I came to the same conclusion as my heavenly Father that Kirby was the one for me. We were engaged eleven months before our wedding day and were married two months before I graduated. Papa God is so good. And, yes, I do love Kirby very much.

If you're looking for a mate, you need to be looking in all the right places. Kirby and I have hosted many Christian couple communication classes. Getting these couples to talk about where they met was not always easy. So, Kirby came up with a spiel that went something like this. "We will start. I met Glenda over a bottle of alcohol and married her while she was at the state mental hospital." That got everyone's attention! It also broke the ice, because some marriages did originate in those settings. I'd chime in later to explain that the alcohol was rubbing alcohol for my newly pierced ears, and the psych rotation in nursing school placed me at the state hospital for three long months. There were no longer boring conversations or silence at our table. Be in healthy places, because it's important.

Write down the qualities you want in a mate. This helps solidify and bring to pass your choice.

It's really important to get to know your potential mate. Kirby and I dated several years long distance. Distance or not, time helps you get to know this person: likes, dislikes, goals, values, beliefs, future plans, and more.

Then, listen when the Lord answers your prayer. He does know *best* and helps you make the right choice.

Here is a list of questions you might want to ask your potential spouse:

1. What are your spiritual beliefs? Do you know Jesus personally? Do you live for Him, or do you just "do your own thing?"
2. Do you know your purpose and direction in life?
3. How close are our values?
4. What are your goals? Do you have a five or ten year plan? Are they written down?
5. Will we both be working? What about employment: work for corporate, be self employed, or be a bum?
6. What about education: attend college, learn a trade, or say *no* to education?
7. How will finances in marriage be managed: his money, my money, our money?
8. Do you have a preference as to where you want to live: in a mansion or on the street, in the city or on a farm, in America or another country?

9. Do you want children or no children? Do you want a small family or a large family? What if we cannot have children? What do you think about adoption? If children, how would you discipline them?
10. Have you been married before? Do you already have children?
11. Do you have debt? If so, how are you getting out of debt?
12. Do you have a criminal record? If so, for what?
13. Are you in good health?
14. Why do you want to marry me? (This had better be good and, for sure, the right answer!)
15. Do you know, that you know, that you know I am the one for you? How do you know? Do you have peace about your decision?

I would be willing to bet money this next question is asked more frequently than not. "Why don't we just live together and try *it* out to see if marriage works for us, see if we are meant for marriage?" In this setting, there is no commitment, no accountability. When asked if he was getting married, I heard my male coworker say, "Why buy the cow if you can get the milk free." Wow! Not only does that opinion set a very low standard for women with no respect or value, it screams no commitment.

In Leviticus 21, God instructs Moses to speak to the priests of the land. Moses is to instruct them on what is expected regarding marriage. Verse 13 states, "And he shall take a wife in her virginity." This is God's *best*. In 1 Corinthians 7:9, scripture points out that if there is no self control, marry. God also wants us to have only one spouse. In Romans 7:2–3, you find that the woman is bound to her husband as long as she lives. When he dies, she is free to remarry. This says one marriage at a time. This makes null and void all the rest of immorality: fornication, adultery, polygamy... God wants you and me to have a marriage with the least amount of hardship. He wants us to have a blessed marriage. He wants marriage to be "on earth as it is in heaven." Heed His word.

I know we all make mistakes, and that's where grace and forgiveness come in. This is where we draw a line to start over. I want to admonish you to stop living in and dwelling on the past, and move on in the present. Stop wearing that coat of shame, bankruptcy, fired, divorce, DWI, harlot, crazy, unwanted, pregnant outside of marriage, or terrible parent because Jesus' blood covers them all. Through confession and forgiveness, our God redeems us and remembers no more. After seeking forgiveness, put on the mind of Christ and start thinking from heaven's perspective.

When we accept Jesus as our Savior and Lord, we become new. Old things are gone; they are no more. When we know Jesus, our behavior doesn't determine our identity; our identity (who we are in Christ) determines our behavior. God's grace is so precious. He says that you're blessed and highly favored. Your creator loves you beyond measure.

To recap:
1. Pray for and about your spouse.
2. Be in the right places.
3. Be the *best* you that you can be.
4. Get to know this prospective mate.
5. Let God choose your spouse.

What do I want in a spouse?
Am I patiently waiting for my mate – or not?

Leviticus 21   Romans 7:2–3
1 Corinthians 7:9

What Does Becoming My *Best* Look Like?

I knew there was much I wanted to include in this section. After all, the *best me*, who I am, is part of our responsiblity on earth. What we do, is the other part. Both of these require decisions or choices which can be right or wrong, good or bad, poor or wise in nature. Let's start from the beginning and take apart man.

Just like the Trinity (Father God, Son, and Holy Spirit), God also made man in three parts: spirit, soul, and body. We're a spirit that has a soul (mind, will, and emotions), and we live in a body (1 Thessalonians 5:23). Most people dwell on the outward appearance and don't give much value or credit to the spirit or the soul. However, the Lord looks upon the heart (1 Samuel 16:7). Therefore, that's where we will start – the heart, other wise called the *spirit man*.

SPIRIT Living well, being the *best* you can be, comes from God's Word. Therefore, we need to be reading the Word, studying the Word, and memorizing the Word to be prepared for life's challenges. We need to be rooted.

In the book, *Rooted*[1], by Banning Liebscher, I learned that to build a root system of whom we trust and the truth itself, we have to grow in three soils: intimacy, serving, and community.

Intimacy with Father God is found in our secret place, our special place of uninterrupted one on one time with our heavenly Father. This is the place where we find out how much we're loved, what our purpose is in life, how our needs are met, and what fruit we're to produce in our lives that will last generationally.

Service is putting our faith and God's love into action. To grow in trust, we must step out. This is accomplished through serving. We grow by putting into action what God's Word says.

Scripture says that God's thoughts are higher than our thoughts. It says that to be great, we must be the least (Luke 9:48). We're to love our enemies, bless those that curse us, do good to those that hate us, pray for those that use us and persecute us (Matthew 5:44). The one of greatest love means laying down one's life for a friend. Serving in weakness brings glory to our God, because it's a sacrifice. I don't know about you, but I know I'm still growing in this area.

Community is the third soil for becoming rooted. This soil teaches us forgiveness. When we do not forsake the assembling of ourselves together, when we find a church to attend on a regular basis, we receive wise counsel and encouragement. We discover that we are a part of Christ's body. Through community, we learn and develop the part God gives us.

Let's stop here and revisit the soil of intimacy for a moment. Before we are rooted through the soils of intimacy, service, and community, we first must know Jesus and have a personal relationship with Him. We need to know who we trust in.

Romans 3:23 says, "For all have sinned, and come short of the glory of God." We're separated from God and His holiness. Romans 6:23 states, "For the wages of sin is death; but the gift of God is eternal life through Jesus Christ our Lord." To remedy this situation, God sent His Son, Jesus, into the world to overcome sin and death by paying the price for the wrongs we've done. "For God so loved the world, that he gave his only begotten Son, that whosoever believeth in him should not perish, but have everlasting life" (John 3:16). We all have to make a choice. "That if thou shalt confess with thy mouth the Lord Jesus, and shalt believe in thine heart that God hath raised him from the dead, thou shalt be saved" (Romans 10:9). Are we going to confess with our mouth the Lord Jesus and believe in our heart that Jesus was raised from the dead, or not? It's a choice.

I love to hear how people find Jesus in their lives. For some, it's a simple "yes"; for others, it might be, "Take my life and do something with it." Others have prayed and asked Jesus to come into their heart (spirit man). For some, it can be, "Forgive my sins and help me be a witness for you." Whatever your words are, they're the most powerful ones you'll ever speak. You just chose to *live in heaven with the Most High God – forever!*

At the moment we receive Jesus, the Holy Spirit comes and resides within us, making us righteous in our spirit, spotless without blemish. We are sealed (Ephesians 1:13). Scripture says that old things have passed away, and all things have become new (2 Corinthians 5:17). We become new. That's where we get the term *born again.* This is *Him in me.*

When we make the decision to believe that Jesus is our Savior, several things happen. Not only does the Holy Spirit come and live in us, but we should no longer see ourselves as just old sinners, saved by grace. We should see ourselves as a new creation, righteous in Christ Jesus. When we become a Christian, we are no longer bound by the law. We are under grace. Hebrews 8:10 states, "...I will put my laws into their mind, and write them in their hearts..." We no longer hold fast to the law for instruction. The Holy Spirit within becomes our instructor.

When the Holy Spirit fills us (Acts 2:4), we can be refueled through a new prayer language, have the Spirit pray for us when we do not know how to pray, and have another avenue to thank and praise the Lord. Being part of the Trinity, the Holy Spirit has access to all knowledge and wisdom. What an amazing blessing! Agree with the Lord today, and change your life forever.

Living for the Most High God is second on the list. This is *I in Him.* Knowing why you were made (purpose) and where you are going in life (direction) are probably the two most important questions people ask themselves. Living for Papa God instead of for self usually answers these questions. "For I know the thoughts and plans I have for you…" (Jeremiah 29:11). Knowing your purpose and direction in life is ongoing and changes from time to time. When seasons change in your life, having an ongoing relationship with your heavenly Father keeps you on the right path.

Hearing our Lord is so very special. He communicates with us through His Spirit, the Word (Bible), and through His creation. Listen and learn. He's a God of variety. His answers come in different forms: opening and closing doors of life events, reading a rhema word, receiving words of wisdom from friends, having a knowing in your spirit, hearing the Lord audibly speak to you, the ministering of music, and having peace in a situation. These are just a few of the myriad ways you can hear from God. It's important to stop talking so much to Him and focus on Him. Don't listen from your head (what you think); learn to listen from your heart (what the Holy Spirit thinks). Our Lord says that His sheep (Christians) know His voice. Since He never leaves us (Hebrews 13:5), He wants to communicate with us.

Listening and following through with what the Lord says, keeps us from sinning. When we follow the Lord, He takes care of us. Matthew 6:33 says, "But seek ye first the Kingdom of God, and His righteousness, and all these things will be added unto you." Here, things refer to food, clothing, shelter, and other essentials for living. We cast our care on Him; we don't "take care." Scripture also says that when we delight in the Lord, He gives us the desires of our heart (Psalm 37:4). If you want to know your purpose and direction in life, delight yourself in Him.

With salvation, we're given the fruit of the Spirit for our lives: love, joy, peace, patience, gentleness, goodness, faithfulness, kindness, and self-control (Galatians 5:22–23). These are to be developed and lived to the fullest. By the way, these qualities do set us apart, and people notice! Let me give you an example so you don't think I'm just making this up.

Our grandson, Josh, lives in Fort Worth. Because of distance, we don't get to see him as often as most of our other grandchildren. However, Josh gets to spend a week in the summer with Nana B and Papa K. His comment to me during one of these visits was, "Nana B, you're the kindest person I know." WOW! I almost cried. It's nice to know that the fruit of the Spirit really is visible.

Before going to the soul, I want to address *faithfulness* of the fruit of the Spirit. Somehow in my life, I've always thought faith had to come totally from me. I would hear people say to me, "Just have faith in God. Just believe God for healing. Just believe God for prosperity. Without faith, you know we cannot please God." I have believed it was all me. I had to muster up faith. I've heard Scriptures on being given the measure of faith, faith coming from hearing the Word of God, and God not being a respecter of persons. I somehow could not "connect the dots." It still seemed to fall on my shoulders. Finally, I realized that I've been given the faith. (It's part of the fruit of the Spirit.) The studying of scripture is to help me become fully persuaded in making the right choice, agreeing and partnering with my heavenly Father.

Just like it's my choice to love the unlovely, to be joyful in hard circumstances, to forgive my sibling, to be patient when I am still standing in line, to be peaceful in stressful times, to have self control when I want to indulge in a second bowl of ice cream, it's my choice to choose faith in agreeing with my heavenly Father. My part is all about *choice,* choosing faith and renouncing doubt.

Becoming fully persuaded converts humanity to divinity, from man's way to God's way. When we agree with God, united faith, He infuses His very life into us empowering us to live on a supernatural plane. It's vertical, and it brings heaven to earth. This truth set me free. I hope it also helps you. Having faith to make wise choices is still another part of becoming the *best* you.

When we get *self* (our strong will) out of the way, it's really a no-brainer to make the decision or choice to serve our strong and mighty Creator – the Almighty God, Elohim. He is our good, good Father that loves us more than we know.

SOUL Let's take a look at the *best* soul: our mind, will, and emotions. (Your brain is part of the body; the mind is part of the soul.) While our spirit is righteous and pure, our soul is quite different. This area of our personhood has to be renewed. This is an on going process and is the area that we struggle with the most. This is the area where our mind learns, processes what it wants to believe as truth, and then makes a decision. We choose; we will it. When Christ is in you (salvation) and you are in Him (doing His will), the soul is transformed more quickly.

So let's apply this to how you see yourself. As an example, what does your self image look like to you? Do you view yourself as a failure, stupid, shy and fearful with no self confidence, a real nobody? Or do you see yourself as your heavenly Father sees you – wonderfully made, intelligent, beautiful in His sight, wise, gifted, special (one of a kind), and much more. Psalm 139:14 states, "We are fearfully and wonderfully made." Genesis 1:26 states, "...Let us make man in our image, after our likeness: and let them have dominion..." I don't know about you, but those words sound like we're pretty important to Papa God.

Coming from the place of learning through pain or amazement, what do you believe (mind)? It's your choice (will). Depending upon that choice, appropriate feelings (emotions) follow – mind, will and emotions.

The next topic that I want to address is that of speech. To be the *best* you, there needs to be the *best* words spoken. What we say (the words we speak) create. Remember back in the garden of Eden? God gave man *authority* over... subdue...multiply... He's never taken authority away from us. Proverbs 18:21 says, "Life and death are in the tongue." Therefore, what we speak is a serious thing. Do you want doom and gloom in your life, or do you want blessing and honor to reign?

In general and without thinking, we have a tendency to be critical and speak lack, sickness, and curses over ourselves and others. For example: "We don't have money for that. We'll never be able to get out of debt. My feet are killing me. That's to die for. I could hug you to pieces. Don't get wet, or you'll catch a death of cold. Take care." I could go on and on.

We should be deliberate in what we say and speak what we want by faith. We should not be flippant about speech like poor jokes, hear say, or complaints. When we speak, we should speak positive, meaningful, encouraging and uplifting words, words you would hear your heavenly Father say. Speak salvation, wisdom, and favor. Create and enlarge your borders. Speak goodness.

Remember, you're a child of the King. We're heirs of the Most High God. We have an awesome inheritance that we can bring down from heaven. When we're in Christ doing the will of the Father, we have the authority, remembering God has the power.

Think of it like this. Take the picture of a light switch and electricity. We flip the switch (agreeing with God by faith); we step out and activate. The electricity (God) is the power. This is a picture of God's power "lighting up," taking care of lack, healing the sick, and removing whatever *mountain* there is to overcome.

Aligning with our heavenly Father, we can do great things. In Him, speak things as if they *are* and choose faith. Faith brings things into the *now*. We operate from a heavenly realm instead of an earthly realm. In heaven, there is no time – it's forever. However on earth, time is for measurement. Let me illustrate bringing heaven to earth into the now through faith. It takes stepping out of your comfort zone to see the impossible happen.

My granddaughter, Mercy, just returned from Kathmandu, Nepal where she experienced two major earthquakes, seven-plus on the Richter scale, and close to two hundred aftershocks. There was much devastation, damage of property, and loss of lives. In one clinic, Mercy and others with Youth with a Mission (YWAM) prayed over two injured men with bone fractures of the arm and leg. Since the nurse had no facility to help them, they were headed for the nearest hospital. During prayer to Papa God (Jehovah-rapha), bright lights from above filled the room, and both men were healed instantly. This is an example of bringing heaven to earth, bringing down our inheritance of healing. The Lord's Prayer talks about God's will being done on earth as it is in heaven. It's speaking what you want by faith into the now. Normally, it takes two to six months for legs and arms to recover fully – not in the now. Now is God's timing.

On the cross, Jesus said, "It is finished" (John 19:30). He's already taken care of everything. We just have to be *in Him* and by faith take with authority in Jesus name. I don't know about you, but this revelation makes me want to shout. I can have heaven on earth now, if I declare (John 16:23) and believe (Mark 11:24) in Jesus' name, the name above all names and our advocate before the Father.

It's important to learn Scripture so that we know what is ours. Scripture is also our weapon, our sword. Remember how Jesus defeated Satan in the wilderness with Scripture? With Him, we can be free from sickness, fear, anger, addictions, poverty or lack, guilt and shame – bondage. Wisdom, prosperity, protection, good health, favor, peace, and more are ours for the taking. Even though God is sovereign, He so wants us to partner with Him.

I want to talk more on taking authority, what it does and does not look like. Since Jesus said that it was finished on the cross, I don't have to ask God to heal so and so from cancer or take away my fear, or my anger.. He took it all, everything, on the cross over two thousand years ago. IT IS FINISHED! So to pray like this is *not* acceptable. "God, if it's your will, please take my fear and anger away. Please heal my cancer, or please deliver me from depression." NO! No! No! We do not go before God in a begging mentality asking for something we already possess. Our part is to take or receive what God has already provided and give Him thanks and praise.

Taking authority looks something like, "In Jesus' name I take authority over fear. It has no place in my life anymore; instead, I have faith. I speak faith in every area of my life, in what I believe, in decisions I make, and in how I see myself! Lord, You said that perfect love casts out all fear and that You've not given us a spirit of fear, but power, love, and a sound mind. Therefore, I stand on faith believing that it is finished. I thank you, Jesus, for taking all sin to the cross with you and conquering fear. Thank you for your precious blood that covers me, and thank you for answering prayers. I praise your holy name; for You, my Lord, are worthy of honor and glory. In Jesus' precious name, I pray. Amen."

Let Jesus fight your battle, instead of you fighting. He has already taken care of the *it* in your life. Boldly, receive what you need.

Healthy speaking is so important. These words are positive and uplifting. They encourage and edify. Healthy words spoken over others should bring them closer to wholeness. We should be thinking, "What would Jesus say in this situation?" As we use words in dealing with every day life, in prayer, and even for edifying self, choose wisely.

By faith, Kirby and I have started our mornings declaring who we are in Christ and agreeing with the Lord on our future. Job 22:28 says, "Thou shalt also *decree* a thing, and it shall be established unto thee: and the light shall shine upon thy ways." Come and see what we mean.

"Yahweh is the God of all gods, King of kings, Lord of lords. He is the provider of all things. He is the healer of all diseases. He is my God and my Father. He calls me son/daughter. We thank you Lord, for life and purpose.

In the name of Jesus, we decree that we see ourselves the way God sees us. We are blessed and highly favored of the Lord, crowned in glory and honor. We are the righteousness of God in Christ Jesus. We are covered by the blood of Jesus. Protection is ours.

We declare by faith that we serve with divine favor, preferential treatment, and supernatural increase. Because of favor, we have battles won which we do not have to fight. Doors are open for us now. No obstacles can stop us; no hindrances can delay us. Impossible situations are coming to fruitfulness in our lives today. Halleluiah!

Lord, you say to remember Your benefits. So we say, Thank you:
1. for forgiving all our sins
2. for healing our diseases
3. for saving our lives from death
4. for crowning us with loving-kindness and tender mercies
5. for satisfying our lives with good things
6. for renewing us like the eagle
7. for executing righteousness and judgment when we are treated unfairly (Psalm 103:2–6)

We thank you Lord, for blessing us so that we can be a blessing to others. PRAISE THE LORD!

In Matthew 18:18, You said that whatever we bind on earth will be bound in heaven, and whatever we loose on earth will be loosed in heaven. Therefore, in the name of Jesus, we believe (Mark 11:24) and declare that Satan and his followers are bound and are not allowed to operate against us, our family, and extended family in any way. None are able to interfere in any of our affairs – physical, spiritual, mental and social. Satan is to return one hundred fold, all that he has taken from us in our lifetime, and do it now!

Scripture says, 'Are they not all ministering spirits, sent forth to minister for them who shall be heirs of salvation' (Hebrews 1:14)? Therefore, we send ministering angels out as God our Father directs to bring us our harvest needed to be debt free and to share with our family, extended family, partners, and those in need.

As we give time, wisdom, products, prosperity, and spiritual direction, it is given back to us one hundred fold, good measure, pressed down, shaken together, and running over (Luke 6:38).

As for our businesses, the Lord provides Kirby and me access to the best network marketing company in existence today, Ariix, the opportunity company (www.ariix.com/opportunity/kkyle). Ariix has the best compensation plan of any network marketing company. Ariix provides the best products for day to day use that improves the health and quality of life for anyone that uses them. God sends us people that want increase. The Holy Spirit prepares their hearts to receive us. When we talk to someone about Ariix and the Ariix products, we're excited and enthusiastic. They know we are sincere. They believe us, and they join us. As we stay in you, our Father, we have phenomenal businesses with associates as many as the stars. PRAISE THE LORD!

We thank you Lord, for mightily blessing WestBow Press (www.westbowpress.com) in every area: customer support, editing, marketing, web design, book sales, timing and so on. This company has more than enough. As we work with WestBow Press, our books are a great hit. Everyone wants a copy because they want a deeper relationship with You and with their spouse. Thanks for giving grace, peace, and joy to all that participate.

Money comes because of all the seeds that have been planted and because of Your blessing. As we go out promoting and speaking, we have all we need: quick and wise words, discernment, protection, confidence, peace, joy, and fruit. We dedicate these books to You, our Lord.

We speak blessing and goodness over our businesses. Our businesses are a haven, because God is over them. Jesus is walking with us, and the Holy Spirit is directing and teaching through us. We bless our clients with spiritual growth, good physical health, and food for the soul. We transfer peace and joy.

We thank you Lord, for the above, believing we receive; we thank you for answering our petition even before we see it.

Now to our amazing and wonderful almighty God who is holy and worthy of all praise, be blessing and honor and glory and power forever and ever.

In Jesus' name, as it is spoken, so it is done. Amen!"

(I hope that was not too much for you.) So what will your declaration be? Make it yours, but be sure you use scripture. God's word is your *seed* for the crop you want harvested.

I'm not saying that we never ask the Lord for something. There are definitely times when we need answers to questions, want to know what His will is on a particular matter, or need wisdom. Just keep in mind that *it* has been finished on the cross, so declare it.

Remember that life and death are in the tongue. Also, positive self talk really works. I can remember hearing a client at work make some comment about me being *only* a PRN (as needed) nurse. Somehow, in his eyes, PRN stood for less than, not as good as the hired forty hour a week employee. Instead of letting small talk get to me, I repeated positive affirmations all the way to the car. Out loud I declared, "I'm an excellent registered nurse. Everyone wants to hire me. I'm a child of the King, greatly loved and highly favored. I'm fearfully and wonderfully made." I went on and on. By the time I reached the car, those negative words spoken over me had no hold or meaning. Heavens! I had a spring in my step and a song in my heart. As I heard an evangelist say, "I've done preached myself happy!"

Declaring, taking authority, and speaking truth over one's life is a must. Be sure your self talk is in alignment with God's Word. We need to speak those things that are of our Lord. In John 5:19, Jesus said, "...The Son can do nothing of himself, but what he seeth the Father do: for what things soever he doeth, these also doeth the Son likewise."

Let's return to prayer for a moment, Prayer and fasting are just another part of becoming the *best* you. Prayer gets the job done. Partnering with God on anything is powerful. Prayer is our way of communicating with Papa God on any subject of concern. Prayer should contain thanksgiving and praise. We should acknowledge our sins. Prayer should contain asking, seeking, and knocking. Remember to declare and use scripture.

I believe God instituted fasting for several reasons. It frees up more time for Him, and it puts our focus on the Lord instead of the next meal. It allows us to hear and understand Him more clearly. For me, fasting is a picture of laying down my life for a short time for my Friend. Fasting should be led of the Lord. In Scripture, different fasts are mentioned. It's important to know why we're fasting, what to fast, and how long to fast. Matthew 6:18 describes fasting as a private matter – a secret matter. No one else needs to know. (It's about rewards.)

The Lord wants us to remember what He speaks. Fasting makes a greater point. During one of my fasts, I remember the Lord saying that *I was to feed His sheep.* Even though those words seemed less important at the time, I never forgot them, and I've seen those words manifest all through my life.

When repentance, confession, and forgiveness are exercised, we're less weighed down, and there seems to be greater access to the Father. I know from serving in the deliverance ministry at my church, repentance, confession, and forgiveness are a large part of setting people free. After forgiveness comes renouncing lies believed and knowing the truth about a matter. Our Lord even said, "And ye shall know the truth, and the truth shall make you free" (John 8:32). Be a forgiving person, and also remember to forgive yourself. I sometimes think that's the hardest person to forgive because "I should have known better" or "I should have seen it coming."

Guilt and condemnation are easy to take on when we see ourselves as failures. Forgiveness may seem difficult to do, but it's so worth it in the end. Forgiveness is a choice we make. It's not made on how we feel about a person. With true forgiveness, our feelings will align with God's intent. Not only is forgiveness an avenue to freedom, it's also an avenue to wisdom.

The world's full of knowledge, but until we have God's wisdom concerning knowledge, not much good can come from knowledge. Having freedom and open communication to hear the Lord clearly on a matter is what some people would say, "It's worth its weight in gold." – priceless. In wisdom come favor, promotion, wholeness, and much more. God is such a good God. Let Him partner with you to be the *best* you can be.

As a side note, don't allow pride to get in the way. Seek forgiveness, admit wrongs, and turn from them. On the other side of things, don't keep the "Thank you" and "job well done," the appreciation and compliments, for self. We run a great risk of being "puffed up." How many times have you heard someone say, "I know." Give those praises to the Lord and stay humble. They are His anyway. Proverbs 16:18 states, "Pride comes before a fall." I don't know about you, but I like to stay standing.

We have covered quite a bit on how we should think (*mind*), what choice we should make (*will*), and how feelings follow (*emotions*). Now is the time to discuss how God made us.

As I was pondering on our bents and our interests toward certain things like science or computers, I wasn't sure if this section would be soul or body. My determining factor was, "If I die, will this part of me stay with my body, or will it go to heaven with my spirit?" Of course, who I am leaves with the spirit, so our bents are part of the soul. When we die, only our bodies remain on earth.

So with that in mind, I want to say that God gave you what you need for the purpose He has for you at this appointed time. "For we are His workmanship, created in Christ Jesus unto good works which God hath before ordained that we should walk in them" (Ephesians 2:10). Since He knew you before the beginning of time, God has had you planned for a very long time. There are *no mistakes* in this world.

Our soul is a unique blend of *giftedness, temperaments,* and *life experiences.* Let's address our *giftedness* first. God has given each one of us special gifts or talents that help us to accomplish tasks in our purpose. These are all unique. These bents may look like a talent in art, music, or sports. You may have a great singing voice. Maybe your mind is brilliant (high IQ); you think creatively, or you exhibit great mechanical abilities. You may have an interest in farming, the sea, plant life, or animals. You may have a gift for giving or a gift of mercy. *Giftedness* comes in all colors, shapes, and sizes. Develop your gifts, your bent. Being established in the giftings you exhibit, use them to give glory to God. It'll give you satisfying fulfillment and great happiness. God's way always wins.

Now let's address *temperaments.* Some years ago, I came across a book that changed my whole perspective on how I viewed people. The book was titled *Personality Plus*[2] by Florence Littauer. I always wondered why some people were so bossy or why others seemed lazy. Why did some have the attitude that everything is a party; why were others so focused on getting the job done?

Florence Littauer believes that all personalities fall into four categories of which we all carry. She also talks about each person being strong in one or two of these traits. These traits have allowed me to see my personality in a different light, and I understand and interact better with others. I hope it does the same for you.

I've learned much from all four personality traits, their strengths and their weaknesses:

1. *Sanguine* These people have a very outgoing personality. They're considered the life of the party. Sanguines are flexible, loving, trusting, and enthusiastic people. They love crowds and deal with people well. Their weaknesses might include being naïve, arriving late to events, and enjoying lots of attention. They tend to exaggerate stories, over commit, and be disorganized.

2. *Choleric* These persons are considered your leaders, your bosses. Cholerics are highly motivated and goal orientated individuals. They exude confidence and independence. Cholerics don't mind correcting wrongs and are willing to take chances. When looking at their weakness, these individuals can come across as insensitive, impatient, know-it-alls. They don't do the "relax" thing very well. Tact is not in their vocabulary.

3. *Melancholy* These self-sacrificing individuals are thinkers. These are the detailed ones. Being serious about doing things right and thorough causes them to

be list makers. They are punctual creatures of habit that love creativity. Their weaknesses include having a lack of self-confidence, not accepting compliments well, being too introspective (critical), and taking things personally.

4. *Phlegmatic* These quiet, kind, patient people are well balanced. They love peace. Phlegmatics are great listeners and make strong mediators. Even though they show little emotion, they care about people. These may not be risk takers, but they have an "iron" will. Weaknesses include decreased enthusiasm and motivation. Phlegmatics are not goal orientated, and they appear lazy. They easily can put *it* off until tomorrow.

In our family, we are a broad mix of all temperaments. Kirby is mainly choleric with some melancholy, I'm dominantly melancholy with phlegmatic. Our daughter, Lauri, is melancholy and sanguine. John, her husband, is mainly phlegmatic. Our son, Jeff, has an equal part of all except sanguine. He married Amy, a sanguine.

Let me demonstrate how these look in an event. Some time ago, I announced that we were going to have a work day at the farm. We would be painting, clearing brush, cleaning, and so on. Before arrival, I had planned the menu for the day and delegated what everyone was to bring. I had a list of those chores that needed to be addressed. When everyone arrived, Kirby jumped into the boss role by letting everyone know what they were to tackle. Jeff worked all day. Lauri and Amy worked a few hours, then they sat down to visit. John helped a while, and after lunch, he took a nap.

Let's apply these personalities to playing a game. The choleric is out to win, or else. Sanguines are just having fun. Melancholy people want to be sure the game is played right, and nobody cheats. Then the phlegmatic wants the game delayed until tomorrow.

From these explanations and illustrations, you have pretty well figured out what temperament(s) fit you. That also means you know some of the weaknesses that need to be improved. You might even speculate what means of employment fits your personality the best: sanguine – public relations, choleric – president of a company, melancholy – medicine or law, phlegmatic – self employed.

Third is *life experiences*. While giftedness and temperaments are internal, life experiences are external. It's pretty obvious that life's experiences help shape who we are. I've heard sayings like: "No pain, no gain," and "If at first you don't succeed, try, try again." Then there is the one, "A smart man learns from his mistakes; a wise man learns from the mistakes of others." How much time and effort we put into something, how we perceive an experience, what we believe is truth, and the choices we make all add up to that unique special you. We learn from pain, and we learn from amazement. Personally, I would prefer to learn from the pleasant and uplifting moments in my life. How about you?

The last part of looking at the *best* you deals with *love languages*. I want to say that we all have a way that we perceive we are loved. Even though this topic can go here, I have opted to put this topic in the next section entitled, What Does Love Look Like?

So, are we there yet? Almost!

BODY Since humanity generally looks at the appearance, how we look on the outside, we need to be the *best* with what God has given us. First impressions are important to the world.

When people look at you, what do they see? We have all heard critical statements like: "Did you see what she was wearing? She must have had a bad hair day! He's really fat, or she's too skinny. He's conceded. She's so stuck up."

While man sees the outward appearance in a worldly judgmental way, God sees your body quite differently. He calls your body His *temple* – His holy place where He resides. Romans 12:1 talks about presenting your body as a living sacrifice, holy and acceptable unto God. This is your gift back to the Lord.

You are His workmanship: you are His representative. 1 Corinthians 6:19–20 states, "What? know ye not that your body is the temple of the Holy Ghost which is in you, which ye have of God, and ye are not your own? For ye are bought with a price: therefore glorify God in your body, and in your spirit, which are God's." When your soul lines up with your spirit and you make wise choices, your body wisely follows. You glorify God in spirit and body. You're created by God, in the image of God, to have a relationship with God and to serve God. I can say, "It's really supposed to be all about God."

For a moment, let's discuss the outward appearance. While cleanliness and proper grooming are pretty self explanatory, I think the *dressing well* needs to be addressed. A bodice too low or too tight and a hemline too short are really not appropriate in representing our holy God. You can call me a prude and not with the times, if you want. However, if you were going out to dinner with Jesus, would you wear what you have on? Be a great representative for your Redeemer. After all, He is with you – always.

Besides good hygiene, we also need proper sleep (seven –nine hours), clean air to breathe, purified water to drink, and proper exercise to maintain a healthy body. Eating healthy foods, taking supplements, and maintaining a healthy body weight all facilitate the *best* you in outward appearance.

When I was growing up, very seldom did you see an overweight person. Obesity has increased greatly over the past thirty to forty years. I'm sure the amount of stress that the corporate world creates has helped. However, let's observe food for a moment.

I attribute much of our over weight status to junk food, sodas, and other processed foods used to save time when we are "on the run." Sugar usage, sugar substitutes, and high fructose corn syrup can suppress the immune system, contribute to diabetes and cancer, and support weight gain. Sugar is added to about eighty percent of the foods on the market today. Food preservatives, food additives, genetically modified organisms (GMO), colors, synthetics, fillers, and parabens have been added to so many foods and products, that the body doesn't know what to do with them. Much is stored in our fatty tissue.

I say all of this to get you thinking about what you eat. Your eating healthy means choosing organic fruits and vegetables. It means eating farm raised or grass fed meats without antibiotics and hormones. Eating healthy cuts down on medical and dental visits, and when you feel better, you're more productive.

I am not going to elaborate on drugs, alcohol, or tobacco. These require no further thought.

There are many books that address eating habits, and more specifically, weight loss. Around every corner you hear of another fad – this diet or that diet. Over the years, I've decided that eating healthy is the only way to keep a healthy weight.

Recently, I discovered Dr. Don Colbert's book, *Let Food be your Medicine*[3]. This Christian author writes about healthy eating through a modified Mediterranean diet and discusses different foods that help in the healing process or in the prevention of certain illnesses like heart disease, diabetes, auto-immune diseases, cancer, Alzheimer's disease, ADHD, mental illnesses, and more. He addresses inflammation and the damage that it can produce if left unchecked. According to Dr Colbert, there are thirty five diseases related to being overweight. Weight loss is a primary topic of his book, discussing hormones, attitude and timing. To stay healthy, our eating needs to be a healthy life style. Choose well. Make a choice to at least work toward a healthy you. The rewards are great.

In Genesis 1:29, God speaks, "...Behold, I have given you every herb bearing seed, which is upon the face of all the earth, and every tree, in the which is the fruit of a tree yielding seed; to you it shall be for meat." Ezekiel 4:9 states, "Take thou also unto thee wheat, and barley, and beans, and lentils, and millet, and fitches, and put them in one vessel, and make thee bread thereof..." Deuteronomy 14:3–21 deals with what meats should and should not be eaten. (To paraphrase here, mainly oxen, sheep, goats, and deer are good meats). "And every beast that parteth the hoof, and cleaveth the cleft into two claws, and cheweth the cud among the beasts, that ye shall eat" (Deuteronomy 14:6). Further along, it says not to eat camel, rabbit, coney, or pigs. Verse nine states, that from the water, "...all that have fins and scales shall ye eat." Somehow, that does not include catfish, shrimp, or crab. Birds are acceptable except the eagle, vulture, raven, owl, hawk, swan, pelican, stork, bat and a few others. The last thing is no eating of sick animals that have died. Okay!

Genesis 6:3 states, "...yet his days shall be an hundred and twenty years." God has stated what long life should look like. What will you choose to help facilitate His *best*? Will you partner with God to see long life come to pass for you? We all have choices to make daily. Make wise ones! As Star Trekkers might say, "Live long and prosper."

Let's recap:

1. spirit
   a. Become rooted.
   b. Come to know Jesus as your personal Savior.
   c. Make Him the Lord of your life. Serve Him.
   d. Be filled with the Holy Spirit, and receive your prayer language.
   e. Know purpose and direction for your life through relationship.
   f. Develop the fruit of the Spirit.
   g. Understand that we are given faith, and our part is studying the Word to have the mind of Christ which produces correct choices.
2. soul (mind, will, and emotions)
   a. Renew your mind through the Word.
   b. Choose life; the words we speak create.
   c. Fast and pray; declare.
   d. Use positive self talk.
   e. Confess and forgive; know the truth.
   f. Seek wisdom and renounce pride.
   g. Develop giftings.
   h. Know temperaments:
      • sanguine
      • choleric
      • melancholy
      • phlegmatic
   i. Learn from life experiences.
3. body
   a. Check outward appearance.
   b. Be a living sacrifice.
   c. Make healthy choices for staying well.
   d. Enjoy healthy eating – or not.

What does your *best* look like?
How do you see yourself? Are any changes needed?

1 Thessalonians 5:23	Job 22:28
1 Samuel 16:7	Psalm 103:2–6
Luke 9:48	John 12:50
Matthew 5:44	Matthew 16:19
Romans 3:23	Matthew 18:18
Romans 6:23	Luke 6:38
John 3:16	John 19:30
Romans 10:9	Mark 11:24
Ephesians 1:13	Hebrews 1:14
2 Corinthians 5:17	John 16:23
Hebrews 8:10	John 5:19
Acts 2:4	John 8:32
Jeremiah 29:11	Proverbs 16:18
Hebrews 13:5	Ephesians 2:10
Matthew 6:33	Romans 12:1
Psalm 37:4	1 Corinthians 6:19–20
Galatians 5:22–23	Genesis 1:29
Psalm 139:14	Ezekiel 4:9
Genesis 1:26	Deuteronomy 14:3–21
Proverbs 18:21	Genesis 6:3
2 Timothy 1:7	Matthew 6:18

What Does Love Look Like?

What is *love*? Is there a difference between infatuation and intimacy? Are there different kinds of love?

Most people really don't know what this word *love* means. Many look for love in all the wrong places. There even seems to be many different thoughts when the word *love* is mentioned. From the world's perspective, it might say love means infatuation, adultery, or pornography.

I have heard love being described as a feeling, an attitude, a decision, and an action. I've even heard it said, "Loving is sharing." From God's perspective, "Love covers a multitude of sins" (1Peter 4:8). God even says that He is love (1 John 4:16).

Let's compare two perspectives of love – infatuation versus intimacy. Each has quite different outcomes or results. You might even call these results *consequences*.

INFATUATION

1. Infatuation is instant desire.
2. It's one set of glands calling to another.
3. Infatuation is covered by a feeling of insecurity. You're excited and eager, but you're not genuinely happy. There are nagging doubts, unanswered questions, and the little

things about your beloved that you would prefer not to examine closely. It might spoil the dream.

4. Infatuation says, "I must get married quickly. I can't risk loosing him."
5. Infatuation has an element of sexual excitement. If honest, you'll admit it's difficult to be together, unless you're sure it will end in sex.
6. Infatuation lacks confidence and trust. When he's away, you wonder if he's cheating on you. Sometimes, you even check.
7. Infatuation might lead you to do things you regret later.

INTIMACY

1. Intimacy is friendship that has caught fire.
2. It takes root and grows day by day.
3. Intimacy is quiet understanding and the mature acceptance of imperfection. It's real. It gives you strength; you support your beloved. You're warmed by her presence. Even when she's away, miles don't separate you. Regardless of distance, you know you can wait.
4. Intimacy says, "Be patient, and don't panic. Plan your future with confidence."
5. Intimacy is mature friendship. You must become friends before you can become intimate.
6. Intimacy carries trust.
7. With intimacy, there are no regrets. Intimacy's an upper; it makes you look higher and think greater. It makes you a better person.

Bible scholars speak of at least three kinds of love:
1. Agape love is God's unconditional love.
2. Phileo love is a friendship love.
3. Eros love is intimacy between husband and wife.

Let's look at each one more closely.

Agape love This is the Father's love for us. God says that His love is unconditional. We cannot earn it. We cannot work for it. It's given to us freely. Godly love is edifying. In a marriage, it would say, "When you hurt, I hurt because you and I are one." It says, "There is nothing you can do or say that will make me love you less." It's a feeling. It's an attitude. It's a choice. Unconditional love involves listening, being thoughtful and considerate, meeting valid needs, and seeking forgiveness without bringing up the past. It does not participate in attacks, accusations, and competition. With regard to the three parts of man – spirit, soul, and body – of course, agape love would pertain to the Spirit.

Phileo love Being close friends reminds me of Jesus walking with us and having a relationship with us. In marriage, that looks like discussing values and belief systems. It's building dreams, goals, and plans for the future together. It's growing in unity, becoming one (being on the same page, so to speak). Here, regarding to the three parts of man, phileo refers to the soul – mind, will, and emotions.

Eros love I kind of equate this form with the Holy Spirit. Since we are spirit beings, when we become Christians, we become one in spirit. Likewise, eros love is the physical union between a husband and wife becoming one. Usually this is the becoming fruitful and multiplying part. Children are the result of God's wonderful design. Yes, you are right concerning eros relating to the body.

Scripture says to love the Lord with all our heart (Spirit) mind (soul) and strength (body). It's only natural to believe a truly healthy marriage also will carry all three forms of love: agape, phileo, and eros.

Next, let's look at ways we as individuals see ourselves loved – our love languages. Yes, there's such a thing. If we were in heaven, we would not be concerned with being loved. However because of the fall of man, humans have a little harder time maintaining this wonderful quality.

From Gary Chapman's book, *The Five Love Languages*[4], I discovered there are five languages:

1. words of affirmation
2. quality time
3. gifts
4. acts of service
5. physical touch

Let's examine each one.

Words of affirmation This is an easy one. Be an encourager. Encouraging words are uplifting, and they move you forward. Words of affirmation could sound like a thank you, a compliment, or a word of encouragement. It may sound like forgiveness; we're not perfect beings. (Please don't keep score.) Most people enjoy others complimenting them or thanking them for a job well done. Words of affirmation are number two on my love language list.

Quality Time This love language is my number one. Quality time is having your undivided attention – no third party, no interruptions, and no changing times. You're looking me square in the eyes. You're not preoccupied with your cell phone, the computer, or television. You're not trying to read a book or fix something when carrying on a conversation with me. This conversation requires listening and focusing on the moment. Quality time may look like taking a trip together, attending festivities together, or sitting on the couch together talking. It does not look like going to a party and abandoning your spouse to talk with peers. Abandonment is not part of quality time.

Because of my German and English heritage, I grew up in a culture with little hugging and kissing. Gifts mainly were for birthdays and Christmas. There wasn't much direct praise and almost no acts of service. However, Mom and Dad invested much one on one time with me. Learning to cook, sew, swim, and oil paint said volumes. Since I played a clarinet in marching band, they attended most Mart High School football games. For someone with the quality time love language, having attention went a long way.

Gifts These gifts are usually gifts of love, which means that they have meaning behind them. People with this love language will display their gifts and talk about them incessantly. They're visible reminders of another's love. Sometimes you can give the gift of self – your presence. Gifts do not always need to be expensive; be creative.

Acts of Service This is *doing something* for someone. You please by serving. There are a myriad of chores that can be tackled around the house: cleaning, manicuring the lawn, going grocery shopping, and repairing broken items. This list could go on and on.

I remember one Christmas I received a little booklet of chores my children would do for me the coming year. Kirby also helps out around the house. I think he has personal reasons for helping. Part of his love language is words of affirmation. He will do something, like change a light bulb or trim the shrubs, and not tell me. Of course, when I find his little escapade, I either thank him or praise him for a job well done. He might even get a hug or two. While acts of service is not my love language, it does serve a purpose for Kirby in his affirming world.

Physical Touch This is a form of showing love emotionally. It appears in different forms as holding hands, kissing, hugs, pats on the back, massages, and intimacy. As you can see, a touch can be short and sweet like a pat on the back or have great magnitude like intimacy. Yes, this is my husband's number one love language. After forty eight years of marriage, we still hold hands when we go places. Almost every morning, Kirby gives me a big hug and a kiss and tells me, "I love you." Then I do the same – undivided attention and affirmation for me, and physical touch and affirmation for Kirby. What a way to start the day! As far as intimacy goes, I consider intimacy between husband and wife to be a very private matter. I truly believe there are different strokes for different folks. So, from the movie, *Forest Gump*, "That's all I'm going to say about that."

It's important that we know we are loved. Married couples need to be aware that they are loved by their spouse. It's crucial for children to understand that their parents love them. Knowing each other's love language even helps us to better understand friends, co-workers, and bosses.

Sooo, what does God say *love* looks like? 1 Corinthians 13 gives us that answer. Paul paints us a picture of what love is and what it is not:

1. He says that without love we become as harsh sounding brass, tooting our own horns with no one listening. Or we are like a tinkling symbol, so quiet that no one hears what is said.

2. If we have all knowledge and faith, the gift of prophesy for edifying, exhorting or comforting, and the understanding of all of God's secrets and mysteries, we are nothing without love.

3. Without love, there is no profit, even if all goods are given to feed the poor or we give the ultimate sacrifice of one's body to be burned (being a martyr).

4. Love looks like the following:
- is long suffering (patient and strong endurance)
- is kind and not rude
- is not envious
- is not selfish – does not insist on having its own way (not prideful)
- is patient and slow to anger
- thinks good
- rejoices in truth and righteousness
- holds up (bears) in all things
- believes the *best* in all things
- hopes all things
- endures all things (sees everything to the end)
- does not fail

Of faith, hope, and love, the greatest of these three is *love*.

Has your picture of love changed?
What is your love language?

1 Peter 4:8   Deuteronomy 6:5
1 John 4:16   1 Corinthians 13:1–13

A Great Marriage Needs a Foundation?

Many people believe that if they're exceptionally good or if they just work hard enough here on earth, they will end up in heaven. However, it's not *what* we do; it's *who* we know. Matthew 7:21–23 states, "Not every one that saith unto me, Lord, Lord, shall enter into the kingdom of heaven; but he that doeth the will of my Father which is in heaven. Many will say to me in that day, Lord, Lord, have we not prophesied in thy name? and in thy name have cast out devils? And in thy name done many wonderful works? And then will I profess unto them, I never knew you: depart from me, ye that work iniquity." As you can see, works doesn't make it. It's *relationship*. It's knowing Jesus personally, walking and talking with Him, learning His ways, seeking His desires, thanking, praising, and worshiping the Lord who has the perfect plan for you.

Just like having Jesus as your Savior and Lord to be the *best* you, it's also the most important ingredient for a strong healthy marriage. In fact, Jesus needs to *be* your foundation. We all find Jesus in different ways and at different stages of our lives.

I became a Christian when I was nine years old. One day in my bedroom the Lord asked me if I would be His. My answer was a simple, "Yes." For Kirby, it was quite different. He was raised in a Christian home and was in church most of his growing up years. However, Kirby liked doing things his way and didn't accept Jesus as Savior until he was in a class called Witness

Involvement Now in the church we attended. In this class, he was asked to write out his testimony. Kirby realized he didn't have one and decided he had better get one before attempting to tell others about Jesus.

Matthew 7:24–27 says that hearing and doing God's will is like a wise man, who builds his house upon a rock. When the rain descended, and the floods came, and the winds blew, and beat upon that house, it didn't fall, because it was founded upon the rock. "And every one that heareth these sayings of mine, and doeth them not, shall be likened unto a foolish man, which built his house upon the sand: And the rain descended, and the floods came, and the winds blew, and beat upon that house; and it fell: And great was the fall of it." The moral of the story appears to be, if you build on the Rock, you will stand. *The Rock!* 1 Corinthians 10:4 says that the Rock is Jesus Christ, the anointed one. So there you have it. Jesus is to be the foundation of your marriage.

A couple that has a relationship with the Most High God and is making choices together through the Holy Spirit is God's way. Otherwise, one might be following *God's way* and the other be following *my way*. Do not be unequally yoked (2 Corinthians 6:14). Obviously, there is no togetherness here. Unity is a must for moving forward with any endeavor. Be in one accord and have a blessed marriage.

The second most important decision regarding marriage is honoring *covenant* in a marriage relationship. This covenant should be a "til death do us part" covenant. This is a decision that's to be taken seriously. *Be sure my spouse to be is the right spouse for me.* Since I have already discussed covenant thoroughly, I won't say any more on this subject. I just want to keep covenant fresh in your mind.

Number three to cover is Genesis 2:24. It says, "Therefore shall a man *leave* his father and mother, and shall *cleave* unto his wife: and they shall be one flesh." What part of leave do you not understand? (I just wanted to get your attention.) Seriously, leaving and cleaving does not mean bringing your mom or dad with you into your marriage. There is no running back home when things don't go your way or there is a misunderstanding with your spouse. There should be no tattling or gossip with parents. You shouldn't expect regular financial support or anything else from Mom or Dad. Cleave means relying on each other to resolve conflict, to support your family, to set your own value system, goals, responsibilities, and so on.

I remember when Kirby and I were first married that we questioned where we wanted to worship the Lord. Even though both of us had been raised in the same denomination, we wanted to decide on our own if that denomination was the place of worship we wanted for our family. We visited all types of Christian churches, and we decided upon one together, the two of us in unity. Oneness happens among God, husband, and wife, not with parents in the mix.

Yes, parents are to be honored and respected, but they are not to be part of your marriage. You're starting your own family now – a new generation.

Number four to discuss is the importance of *love*. Love comes in different forms. Besides the obvious of sexual intimacy, love manifests in so many other ways. Loving my husband may be in the form of honor, honoring Kirby for who he is. I want him to see himself as the *King* of our household. Since God said that the man is the head of the home, I should honor the fact that he carries the authority to make final decisions (1 Corinthians 11:3). For me, love looks like security.

Love may appear as appreciation – appreciation for accomplishments made, dreams fulfilled, tasks completed. Love may look like listening without "fixing it" or being judgmental. Standing by our spouse's side when life gets tough can say love. Love can look like correction or a second opinion (constructive criticism). It may sound like, "I was wrong. Please forgive me." Forgiveness is huge for any marriage, because no one is perfect. Remember, love covers a multitude of sins.

Just as important as love is in a marriage, so is the element of trust. *Trust* is number five of the marriage foundation. Being trustworthy – no lying – is a very important ingredient in the foundation of a marriage. Your foundation needs to have trust to maintain peace and harmony. Trust is fragile. It takes time to develop a trustworthy relationship and seconds to destroy it. Protect trust.

Trust is a belief and reliance on something or someone without questioning. I cannot remember a time where I have not trusted Kirby. He is a man of his word. Since keeping his word is so important, Kirby seldom makes promises. Lying is not his thing; his integrity is important.

Because Kirby and I believe in covenant, we agreed from the start that there would be no other in our relationship. We would be faithful to each other. With that final choice having been made, no other decisions on the matter ever have to be made over and over. The answer is always the same. Being true to one another has kept me from wondering what Kirby is doing when he calls and says he has to work late at the office. This is trusting *horizontally*.

Believing God without doubt is trusting *vertically*. Even though we let our Lord down, He never lets us down. He is an alive God who never leaves us nor forsakes us. He loves us unconditionally;

He even directs us. Proverbs 3:5–6 admonishes us to "Trust in the Lord with all your heart and lean not unto thine own understanding. In all thy ways acknowledge him, and he shall direct thy paths." Here is another covenant our Lord makes with his people.

It's been observed that all kinds of physical and verbal abuse as well as abandonment issues have caused individuals to mistrust others. Mistrust presents as assumptions, judgments, putdowns, jealousy, and stalking. If this is an area that needs resolution, please seek help. Forgiving self and others and becoming free of lies are paramount. The truth does set us free (John 8:32).

God does not make robots. He created us all uniquely, at the right time and for a specific purpose. We think differently, and we choose differently. As a married couple, we're not the same in thinking or doing one hundred percent of the time. We're not going to agree on everything. However, being of like mind, there is a solution with God. The Lord can give us an answer for every division in our marriage relationship. We just need to ask, seek, and knock – then *listen* to what Papa God has to say.

Let's recap:
1. Jesus is your Savior and Lord and partners with you in your marriage.
2. Covenant is important.
3. Leave your father and mother and cleave to each other.
4. Love is the greatest; love never fails, and it covers a multitude of sins.
5. Trust is a must.

**What does your marriage foundation look like?
How can *it* be improved?**

Matthew 7:21–23

Matthew 7:24–27

1 Corinthians 10:4

2 Corinthians 6:14

Genesis 2:24

1 Corinthians 11:3

Proverbs 3:5–6

Matthew 22:37

John 8:32

What if We Are Total Opposites?

How do total opposites become one in a marriage relationship? Is this even possible? I want to assure you that the answer is *yes*.

Often we see television advertisements for online dating. Dating services started out being generalized and then moved into specialized ones like those for Christians, farmers, singles over fifty, and so on. Having listened to someone that has tried these services, questionnaires had to be filled out on compatibility. What are your strengths, likes, and goals? What do you want in a person? (Usually that is what you have in common.) How can we be alike? Please do not get me wrong. I'm sure for some, this method of finding a mate has been a success. I just want you to see the other side of the coin, so to speak.

I've discovered some differences in the makeup of men and women. A man's usually logical; he is the solution finder. A man seems to be more motivated when he believes he's needed. The man's basic need is love and affection. The woman, on the other hand, is considered an emotional person that needs to vent. She's motivated when cherished, and her basic need is security. Let's see.

Many have heard the adage that "opposites attract." I'll tell you that Kirby and I are total opposites – *totally*! That may be a bit of an exaggeration, but after I've explained myself, I'm sure you will see the same picture.

When I first met Kirby, I saw him as an introvert, a thinker, but the more I was with him, he became more open. No sharing changed to some sharing. I really thought English was his first language, but he tells me he speaks *Texican*. I'm not sure the Texans that I know would agree.

I've become an interpreter of the English language. Kirby has a whole different vocabulary from the normal English speaking community. For instance, in dealing with our Shih Tzu, Lady, she's beautimus. When brushing her, Lady's front paws are hands, and her back legs are hinders. If she scratches, she's scritching. By the way, fleas are runners, and her collar is her necklace. That's just a few with Lady.

In conversation with grandkids recently, Chick-Fil-A was Fillet of Chicky. Letters can be omitted, changed, or added as in samich for sandwich and sloup for soup.

Then there is the total unknown such as referring to vehicles from the past – the expression of four/sixty. This was explained as air conditioning by four windows rolled down going sixty miles per hour. I was totally lost on that one.

Recently, a friend was over discussing her need for some wood to be cut. Kirby brought out a box and declared he had a board shortner, at which time we proceeded to question him. We had no clue what he was carrying. To relieve your curiosity, it was a circular saw.

When our children were at home, Kirby would tell a joke. This joke would have to be interpreted before we could even consider laughing at it. I don't know if that made it funnier, or if that took the punch out of it. We started calling them Daddy jokes. We all knew what that meant.

When our kids were elementary age, any trip we took included stopping at markers along the side of the road to have a little Texas history thrown in. Kirby would call the historical markers *hysterical markers*. It was years before our children understood they were historical.

This is just a taste. Like I said, Kirby calls it Texican. I won't tell you what I call it. Since we have been married forty eight years, I should be a pretty good interpreter by now, except he's always adding to the list. Knowing what he is saying and knowing what he means can be two totally different things.

Kirby's blessed with a very high IQ and is right handed. He tends to function from a logical point of view. Kirby's a born leader. He's been a project manager much of his career and is computer savvy. His first assignment in nineteen sixty seven was writing a computer program for the National Aeronautics and Space Administration (NASA) in Houston. You remember he's mainly choleric which says, "I'm boss. I have the right answers." Kirby's a very detailed person; he may tell you over and over again to make sure you *get it*. He'll take you to a destination three different ways, because he can. Being very mechanical, he's excellent at repairing just about anything; he focuses on function. Does it work? However, focusing on being punctual is not a priority. Remember, his love language is physical touch. There you have Kirby Kyle.

My picture does not even come close to Kirby's. I have an average IQ, and I'm left handed. I enjoy simplicity. Since I don't know much about function, I tend to move toward how something looks (form). Is it aesthetically pleasing to the eye? I like things done right the first time. Being on time, punctual, is important to me. My qualities of patience, dependability, and organization place me in a serving capacity. Being a registered nurse has been my field of service. I'm creative, and I have enjoyed taking care of our home, training our children to become productive adults in our land of the free. Investing into my grandchildren's lives also is important to me. I would rather shoot the computer than master it, and I'm very directionally challenged. I have been known to enter a store and come out wondering from which way I just came. If you remember, my love language is quality time (one on one with undivided attention). There you have Glenda Kyle.

As you can see, Kirby and I are at opposite ends of the spectrum. At first we really struggled to find anything we enjoyed doing together or some interest we had in common. Kirby liked checking out cars, so I tagged along just to spend time with him. I enjoyed homes, so we would visit open houses and model homes. That satisfied my creative itch. We probably watched many more football games at home than movies at the theater, but who's counting. We really struggled to find common ground. This slowly changed as we started making purchases together, having children together, and serving the Lord together.

We work very well together in whatever goals we set. Kirby leads, and I see that a superior job is accomplished. Whether it is working together being self-employed or serving in ministry, we make a great team. The qualities we exhibit are like bringing different parts of the puzzle to the table to make a glorious picture of success.

God makes us all different. We're one of a kind masterpieces for His purpose at this specific season. We need to embrace who we are and pursue that purpose. Wishing we're different than how God made us or wanting to be like someone else is being less than.

I guess I should add that Kirby and I do have the same belief system and values; our moral code is mostly the same. We give honor and glory to our Lord who is first in our lives. We're trustworthy, dependable, and hard working. We believe in integrity, doing the right thing, and honoring life. Both of us have a servant's heart.

These qualities and values help us tremendously as we move forward and step out to do God's purpose. We've found out that our greatest togetherness is with God things. We study and discuss scripture together from reading our Bibles and from watching Christian television programs. Kirby and I have attended couple Sunday school classes, taught together in marriage seminars for eight years, and held marriage intimacy classes in our church. Over the past few years, I've helped support Kirby in our health and wellness business, and he manages the computer transfers of my manuscripts to publishers. We've served as house parents in a maternity ministry, working with homeless pregnant women. Then Kirby moved to the financial arena of the ministry, and I landed in the adoption agency. We've enjoyed building three bedrooms onto the family cabin – the same project, just performing different duties.

Can you see how much more can be accomplished for His kingdom when we're different and come together to accomplish a God given goal? Unity needs to be the name of the game when pursuing any goal – personal, intimate, business, and social, or in serving, giving, and ministering.

It's been said that two horses together can pull at least three times as much as one by itself. Being of one mind, unified, much more can be done serving others and our Lord. Paul, writing to the church in Philippi states, "Fulfil ye my joy, that ye be likeminded, having the same love, being of one accord, of one mind" (Philippians 2:2). Being unified brings more than strength. Unity brings peace and joy. Yea unity!

Now, how do you feel possibly being married to an opposite?

Philippians 2:2

How Do I Resolve Conflict?

After seeing the previous topic of total opposites, I'm sure the topic of disagreements came to the forefront of your mind. It has mine. Therefore, let's discuss this topic of conflict.

Pondering my marriage, I recognize some criteria for decreasing the quantity of conflicts over the years:

1. Kirby and I try to stay at the same level of spiritual growth.
2. We pray and declare regularly.
3. We state our love to each other regularly.
4. We communicate and resolve conflict quickly.
5. We maintain a yearly goal setting.
6. We accept each other and try not to change the other.
7. We determine to stay focused.
8. We don't take our marriage for granted; it's not a "grab it and bag it" deal.

The first three, I've already addressed or will address at a later time. Let's start with communication that hopefully leads to resolving conflict.

In the past, Kirby's mode of addressing issues when they arose was *don't rock the boat*. Mine used to be *the silent treatment*. You can see that nothing would ever be resolved if we didn't make a conscious effort or set it a priority to step beyond how we feel and address the division. Our unity, our oneness, is more important.

Communication is necessary for decreasing conflicts. Let's examine this topic for a moment. When two become one in marriage, what hurts one also hurts the other. So it's important to be of one mind in whatever is going on in one's marriage.

I've always believed that Kirby and I have had a good marriage, but not a great one. The adage, "If you stop peddling a bicycle, you fall off," can also be applied to marriage. If we stop wanting improvement in our relationship and loose site of its importance, we slow down progress. Some marriages stop functioning healthily. Couples can become married singles, two people living in the same house but who are living very separate lives. Marriages even can crash, causing the end to be divorce.

I've always wanted a healthy marriage and am frequently looking for ways to enhance our relationship. When I heard about a couple communication weekend, I jumped at this idea. I figured, if nothing else, I would have a weekend away with my husband without children. At the time, those moments seemed few and far between. Little did I know that we would come to understand each other better, which in turn would allow us to become closer as a couple.

Kirby and I learned these concepts:
1. God doesn't make junk.
2. Feelings are neither right nor wrong; they just are.
3. The issue is not the issue.
4. Love is a decision.
5. Loving is sharing.
6. Love isn't love till you give it away.

I can hear it now. "Oh no, here come feelings." Yes, *feelings*.

Before we move on, let's examine this word. I sometimes think that feelings have been given a bum rap. I believe that we should have control of our feelings, not allowing them to rule. I believe feelings should stay balanced – no numbing, minimizing, or magnifying. I hear much stated about not making decisions based on feelings, and I agree. However, if feelings are neither right nor wrong, then what we do determines the right or wrong – our actions.

In scripture, it tells us that we're made in the image of God. So was Jesus. We're told that Jesus wept over Lazarus' death, and He was angry (righteous anger) in the temple over the money changers. Spiritually, God is love, and the fruit of the Spirit is love, joy, peace... It all has to do with feelings. Looking at the soul, (mind, will, and emotions), God must have thought feelings were important for us. Otherwise, He would not have created us with emotions. In reference to the physical body, feelings tell us when danger is near and if something is too hot or too cold. I'm trying to say, "Don't discard feelings." Learn to use emotions the way God intended for them to be used. There needs to be a *balance*.

When we believe something, our attitude determines which feelings follow. For example, do you hate snakes because they can bite and possibly poison you, or do you love snakes as a pet? Whatever attitude we perceive, appropriate feelings follow.

We can minimize feelings or over exaggerate feelings. We can reason them away, generalize, personalize, and even deny them. We can hold on to them for years or dismiss them quickly. The demonic realm even can work through feelings – usually fear or anger – when we believe a lie.

Kirby and I discovered in some areas of our lives, we were married singles. We wanted more for our marriage. When writing love letters was introduced, I was sure some of our seminar buddies weren't very excited about this opportunity. For me though, this really sparked my attention. You see, a letter was the catalyst for Kirby and me dating and eventually getting married.

We learned how to share feelings with acceptance instead of believing one of us would be rejected or just tolerated. Our letters needed to begin with affirming our spouse, then state the question, describe the feeling, and end with an endearment.

We discovered there were several ways to describe feelings:
1. Use the five senses of sight, sound, taste, smell, and texture.
2. Use physical sensations.
3. Use colors.
4. Use nature examples.
5. Use examples from past events.

An important part of this letter was to share only feelings – *no explaining why and no problem solving.* This letter was only for the purpose of understanding my spouse. We were to choose our strongest feeling to share. We were reminded again, that there was no conflict more important than our marriage relationship.

There were many topics from which we could choose our question – children, marriage, money, relatives, relationship with God, sexual intimacy, time, work, death, health, and on and on. The list was endless.

Here are some of the questions we chose for writing:
1. Do I like myself, and do I think others like me? How does that make me feel?
2. How does it make me feel, knowing I wasn't consulted on the purchase of a microwave, since we were to agree on any purchase over twenty five dollars?

3. How does not being on time (punctual) to appointments make me feel?
4. When I'm left standing alone at your annual office party while you're conversing with peers, I feel ___.

To help understand this technique, here are a few illustrations. I'm forgoing the affirmation at the beginning and the endearment at the end. Let's take a look at some of Kirby's and my letters on shared feelings of different topics to help you learn this technique.

Improving our relationship

Kirby – "Thinking about improving our relationship makes me feel *expectant*. It looks like a small flicker of a newly started fire in our fireplace and smells like peach cobbler as I step into the kitchen."

Glenda – "When I think about improving our relationship, I feel *loved*. Love looks like a dozen red roses. It tastes sweet like chocolate. Loved is how I feel when I have undivided attention."

Working late

Kirby – "When I think about having to work late at the office, I feel *brokenhearted*. Brokenhearted tastes like salty tears. It sounds like taps playing, and is the same feeling I had as I watched 'Ole Yellar' shot due to rabies."

Glenda – "When you have to work late, I feel *pained*. It sounds like a slap in the face. It tastes like bitter medicine and has a throbbing sensation. It's the feeling I had when our daughter cried for me to stop as I sponged down her high fever."

Saying "no"

Kirby – "When you say 'no' to sexual intimacy, I feel *dismal*. Dismal tastes like black unsweetened coffee when I was expecting sweet hot tea. Dismal looks like our dog whining at the back door with snow dripping from his fur. It was the feeling I had when I accepted the fact that my job would be moving us twelve hundred miles away from home."

Glenda – "I felt *anxious* thinking about this question for dialogue. Anxious looks like our children jumping up and down trying to get my attention. It's the same feeling I had in college while waiting for grades to be posted."

Glenda – "When I say 'no' to sexual intimacy, I feel *annoyed*. Annoyed is red like the red cape of a matador. It sounds like a stuck car horn. It's the same feeling I have when I have to continually remind the children of their chores."

Motorcycle

Kirby – "When I think about my motorcycle in the driveway, I feel *exhilarated*. It smells like chocolate chip cookies fresh out of the oven and tastes like your coconut pie. Exhilarated looks like an eagle soaring over the river and sounds like a large choir singing Handel's *Messiah*. It reminds me of how I felt when we were zipping across the snow in a snowmobile on the plateau of the Rockies in Winter Park, Colorado."

Glenda – "When I think about the motorcycle in the driveway, I feel *grieved*. My grieved feeling is colored red like blood and smells harsh like strong exhaust fumes. It sounds like weeping for a loved one that has just passed away. It's how I feel when I think about loosing my best friend."

After exchanging letters and reading them, we discuss whether we understand each other's feelings – our mate's heart. Our goal is to feel the feeling of our spouse to the extent that the other is feeling it. If one of us has not taken on that feeling, more investigating back and forth is needed. Please remember, only share feelings. Be sure to take the little word *you* out of your sharing. The focus is not your spouse. It's about feelings on the situation at hand. Do not use *because* in your letter to explain why, and please do not problem solve. After sharing feelings and understanding them, the *whys* and the problem solving can begin. Issues never seem quite as important or as volatile after understanding your mate's heart. You've got this, right? Do not underestimate the value of love letters!

Painting word pictures for understanding has been around for a very long time. In Genesis 22:17, God tells Abraham that he will greatly multiply his seed as the stars of the heavens and as the sand on the seashore. David uses this method in Psalm 42:1 where he relates a deer panting for water to his soul hungering after God. Proverbs 19:13 compares a nagging woman to a constant drip. Jesus uses this method for explanation. In the parable of the sower, Jesus uses nature, the sowing of seed, to describe different hearts and what they produce. Jesus even uses the bread and cup to represent a picture of His body sacrificed for us and His blood spilled out for us. Pictures help us remember and encourages us to make wise choices.

After understanding each other's feelings on an issue, the question *Why?* can be discussed. Finding resolution to the matter usually is next. Hopefully resolution will not seem as volatile. With understanding each other's feelings, that is the goal.

Before we even get into the *conflict resolution*, I want to say that there's absolutely no place for any form of abuse. Verbal abuse such as yelling or even rage is inappropriate when approaching a matter. No resolution is accomplished when the focus has become who can yell the loudest. The same goes for being destructive and throwing objects. Find a calm, quiet place where the conflict can be the focus. Be fair, stick to the subject, and finish the fight. Holding hands seems to help keep focus. It also adds a different dimension to the situation. Being manipulative, bringing up the past, name calling (character assassination), and blaming the other person are not allowed. These are not part of solving the issue.

Focus needs to be on the conflict and how it can be resolved. Address the issue. Do not attack the person. There are two sides to every story; hear both sides without interrupting your spouse.

Scripture talks about not letting the sun go down on your anger. Therefore, always bring issues out into the open *quickly*. That way, Satan has no ammunition, and he usually flees.

In the end, have a solution; this stops reoccurrences and brings unity. In the end, compromise, agreeing to disagree, or total resolution is reached. Usually forgiveness is required to set both parties free of any baggage that may want to follow.

I have to admit, there have been times that I have totally disagreed with Kirby on an issue. After discussion, sometimes several times, we have agreed to disagree. Now, I have a choice to make. Since Kirby is the head of the house, I can show him respect and walk through the consequences with him (good or bad), or I can say to God, "sic 'em" and let Him settle the issue. (Remember the third person of your marriage.) I have done both.

I can remember times, especially at the beginning of our marriage, when I believed Kirby just should *know* without me having to tell him. Assuming was frequent. *Do not assume.* It gets you into trouble more than not. Your spouse is not a mind reader; believe me. Your spouse doesn't know what you're thinking. Kirby and I often repeat what the other person has said just to make sure we heard correctly.

Also, do not commit your spouse to a project, a dinner party, or anything else without asking first. Calling your wife on the way home from work to announce that you're bringing home a dinner guest does not win friends and influence people. This definitely will bring unnecessary contention. I hope these tidbits help improve your communication.

I want to admonish you to stop playing games in your marriage. Games only cause conflict, hurt your spouse, and bring division. According to David and Teresa Ferguson's book, *Intimate Encounters*[5], which I highly recommend, I learned that there are six games that need to be eliminated:
- blame game
- procrastination
- nothing's wrong
- martyr
- never enough
- excuses why

Eliminate games! Please!

It seems that when we are under more stress, conflicts are easier to occur. Just coming home from work is not the most appropriate moment to address an issue. Holidays and special occasions also can be stressful times.

Let me give you an example from last Christmas. As part of Kirby's Christmas present, I decided to buy a key rack on which he could hang all of his keys. He was placing keys on wall hangings, the washing machine, and any other place of his choosing. Sometimes, Kirby didn't know where he had put them last.

Out shopping, I found a rack that I thought was very functional. Then, there were a set of play keys that seemed to accent his key rack. I decided to buy both, the rack for him and accent keys for him too (even though that part was for me).

Kirby liked the key rack, but he couldn't understand why I bought the accent keys. From his perspective, he had keys for the rack. My dear husband decided to forgo hanging the fake keys. As I suggested how to hang it *all* on the wall for the proper look, I hear, "I think that they just should be thrown into the brown trash can."

Now to me, that came across as an attack – mean. I could understand Kirby thinking the keys were unnecessary, but throwing them away came across as, "You don't matter. Your creativity isn't important to me."

When addressing the issue, Kirby had no clue that he offended me. His focus was on the functionality of the rack. He believed that the gift was all his to do with as he pleased. The decisions were his to make. My creativity of the wall design had not crossed his mind. If he had known the keys were really mine, his perspective would have heen quite different. His response would have changed. As he mounted the key rack on the wall, his harsh choleric self would have carried more tact. There would have been more discussion.

You will find most issues have an underlying cause. The conflict usually has a personal attack attached to it, and a lie is believed. I hope you realized that the keys were not the issue. The lie was that I believed my idea or opinion didn't matter; it was personal, not material. The truth was that Kirby was oblivious to the offense. He believed he had the say over his gift: he wasn't trying to dishonor me. He just didn't know the whole story.

After sharing both sides and coming to an understanding, we hugged. Getting through this disagreement restored peace and harmony. It's worth resolving conflict.

Kirby is working on being more tactful and less blunt. Me? I'm still dealing with guarding against taking things so personally. P.S. I'm not going to buy Kirby any more gifts that should be mine. The lesson is learned.

Resolving conflict allows us to grow and move forward. Otherwise we are stuck at the issue. Division occurs, and peace and harmony stop.

Remember the scripture, "And ye shall know the truth, and the truth shall make you free" (John 8:32)? This should be the motto for everyone who wants to stay out of bondage and who wants oneness in marriage. It really does work.

Here are two exercises that can bring you closer to your spouse:

1. Both of you choose three of your intimacy needs from this list: respect, acceptance, approval, attention, comfort, security, support, encouragement, affection, and appreciation. After choosing your three, answer this question. How can my spouse meet my top three intimacy needs? Then share your answer with your spouse. I want to preface this. God is the only one that can *totally* fulfill your needs, but He does use us to accomplish His agenda.

2. The second exercise consists of sharing with each other the five strengths or positive character qualities you see in your spouse. When focusing on strengths instead of weaknesses, the ugly seems to diminish.

In today's culture, it's easy to become complacent in marriage because the world has such a low standard for marriage. I challenge you to seek out healthy Bible based teachings like marriage seminars, intimacy classes, and books on marriage. These will improve and grow your godly marriage. It's worth it.

Let's move on and look at *goal setting*. If we don't set goals, how do we know where we're going? Goals set our course. These goals may be short term goals or long term goals of five, ten, and twenty years. God may detour and even change them here and there, and we may chase a rabbit or two. However, more will get accomplished if goals are set in place. The Lord even states, "Where there is no vision, the people perish" (Proverbs 29:18).

According to *Intimate Encounters*[6] by David and Teresa Ferguson, I learned that there are eight areas to consider when setting goals:
1. spiritual growth
2. marriage
3. family
4. household
5. financial
6. career
7. personal and social
8. ministry

Spend some quality leisure time pondering these eight areas. Ask the Lord for His input. These goals should be personal goals for each one in the family as well as for the family as a whole. Be very thorough and specific. *Write your goals down.* If you answer the questions *how* and *when*, most likely these goals will get accomplished. Please don't stop there. Get a calendar, a large one, and place your goals in the appropriate space to solidify your plan of action. Due dates help us stay focused. Have fun with this, and be creative. It'll surprise you how much more can be accomplished when planning is applied to your lives.

It's also an opportune time to look at our *priorities* in life. Where is God in my life? Is He number one in all things? Where do I need improvement? Is family number two? Where do work, ministry, recreation, rest, and others line up?

There was a time in my life that I was ill much of a year. Having been to the same physician multiple times, he asked me to list my priorities. Since he was an urologist, that kind of surprised me. I prioritized what I thought was a "right on" list. When I reviewed with him, he asked me where I was on the list. I told him that I wasn't on the list. His reply was, "That's the problem." I played the martyr very well. Everything and everyone came before me. I say all of this to make a point that we're human. Our bodies have limitations. Know what yours are. Put yourself on that priority list. Life runs much smoother when we're healthy.

Kirby and I make it a yearly event at the beginning of the year to set goals in every area of our lives. We go to the family farm, where there are no phones, televisions, or computers. This creates a distraction free weekend of peace and quiet for us. Find your spot; make it happen.

The last three criteria mentioned for decreasing the quantity of conflicts come from you. Enough has been said that *trying to change your spouse does not work,* and you're pretty much on your own when it comes to *staying focused* and *not taking your marriage for granted.* These are disciplines that demand constant awareness and self-control. These might require placing something on the refrigerator or on the mirror in the bathroom for a constant reminder that your marriage is a priority. Ask the Lord for answers and help. He'll answer you. Whatever it takes, it's worth the price.

What changes do we make to improve conflict resolution?
What goals do we need to set?

Genesis 1:26

John 11:35

Matthew 21:12–13

Genesis 22:17

Psalm 42:1

Proverbs 19:13

Mark 14:22–24

John 8:32

Proverbs 29:18

I Need to Have a Servant's Heart? What about Me? What about Me? What about Me?

When I think about having a servant's heart, I often think back to Jesus. He was the master at meeting other's needs. He taught in the synagogue and on the hillside, fed many people, healed those along the way of leprosy and infirmity, raised the dead, provided wealth for the newly weds by turning water to wine, and supplied Peter more fish than he could possibly haul into his fishing boat. Jesus even restored peace on the sea by calming the wind and the waves. We're to be like Christ. Yes, we are to have a servant's heart.

Remember, we discussed being rooted through service, growing according to Scripture. Serving others not only meets a need, but it also grows us in becoming more like our Lord. I hope you know that serving is not just limited to the community. It starts at home.

I am reminded of the movie, *Fireproof.* This movie is a great illustration of how totally serving your spouse can change a marriage. When control and bickering are changed to serving and caring for your mate, you'll see a huge difference in marriage. Many times a spouse will change or reevaluate a situation because of what he/she has observed. Placing service into a poor marriage can help develop a healthy one. When sharing acts of love with your spouse, poor attitudes usually end up changing to positive uplifting ones on both sides. (You usually receive back what you give.) However, someone has to initiate the process. The results of serving another can be peace, harmony, and unity, not to mention appreciation, love, joy, and grace.

It's important that your mate is free to be the person whom God has intended. I don't have to ask the question, "What about me?" because Kirby let's me be me.

I hope you notice that being a servant is about *you* changing. It's not about trying to change your spouse. You cannot change others, only yourself. It's about becoming the *best* you possible in your marriage. You are responsible only for your actions, not your spouse's actions. Do not take on your mate's stuff. It's not yours. You're only responsible for your personal sins.

There is no need to worry about self. The Lord talks about taking care of us. To paraphrase Matthew 6:25–33, Jesus is saying not to worry about what we eat or drink or wear. Consider the birds. They don't sow or reap. Yet God takes care of them. Then there are the flowers. They don't toil or spin. Yet they give great beauty. Aren't we more valuable than birds and flowers?

We're not to think about food, drink or clothing – needs. God knows that these things are necessary. Verse 33 gives us our answer: "But seek ye first the Kingdom of God, and His righteousness, and all these *things* shall be added unto you." This is the abundant life here on earth. This is the *Him in me* and the *I in Him*. This is being righteous, in right standing. Focus must be taken off of self and placed on Him, being like Him and serving for Him. Our part is staying in His will and fulfilling that will. So, don't fret – REST.

Giving is fun. It comes in different forms; it may look like money, time, ability, or prayer. It may exhibit the qualities of listening, organizing, taking responsibility, or being creative. Giving comes in many flavors. It may be something simple like writing a love note or sending a card. Find out what your spouse needs. Get a list of things that would please your mate and randomly make your service a surprise. Be helpful to a family member or pet. Incorporate your children into your activities. Serve by pampering. Take your mate out on a date (without children) for no apparent reason. You can clean the kitchen after dinner, take phone calls, or give a back rub, to name a few. Serving your spouse doesn't have to be a monumental occurrence. What's important is that giving of yourself means something special to the other person. You are giving from the heart, not out of duty. Be a giver, not a taker.

My most favorite blessing from Kirby is his making coffee and setting the timer for perking just as I get up and face the morning. Smelling fresh brewed coffee every morning that I did not have to make is super special to me. It says, "I love you." When Kirby gives me a hug and a kiss every morning and tells me that he loves me, that has security, protection, and peace written all over it. Be a servant!

Do you have a servant's heart?
How do we serve?

Matthew 6:25–33

What about our Finances?

Deuteronomy 28:12 states, "...and thou shalt lend unto many nations, and thou shalt not borrow." In Romans 13:8, we're told to owe no man anything but love. What huge statements!

I have not known anyone in my whole life time that started out in marriage with no debt. Having student loans, starting one's own business, needing a better job to support the family, and mounting medical bills are just a few of the reasons why debt occurs in marriages. The list can go on and on in making poor choices concerning money. Standing on the above Scriptures, I believe we agree that debt needs to be eradicated.

Over the years, Dave Ramsey has been a great teacher in helping those like you and me find financial freedom and prosperity. In his book, *The Total Money Makeover*[7], Ramsey talks about letting money work for you to accomplish being debt free.

I've learned that like anything that needs to be fixed, there needs to be the reality that something is broken. Couples should view their financial situation as bondage that needs to be remedied. In this instance, it's real easy to play the blame game and not take responsibility for one's own actions. There needs to be a "come-to-Jesus" meeting on this challenge and admit drastic measures need to take place. The "I want it now" mentality has to go. Unity has to be the name of the game. This *game* requires persistence, patience, consistency, and self-control.

I want to interject here, that when we borrow money to pay for items large or small, we have just made a covenant with the world to meet our needs instead of looking to God for provision. We need to break this covenant that was made over our finances and move on with the Lord for debt cancelation, increase, and promotion. Blessings come in many forms; God has the best answers.

Let's start with a budget. Yes, a *budget* is necessary. We need to live within our means. How else can we determine where we are financially? Write down every area that requires money. Compare the total with your couple income. Usually, if there is more month than income, eating out, entertainment, and frivolous buying are the first items to go.

For many years, I've heard the statement that we cannot keep doing the same thing over and over and expect to get different results. In other words, if you want change in your finances, there has to be change in action.

Some steps to financial freedom may look like:
1. paying off a mortgage on a home in fifteen years instead of thirty years
2. paying with cash instead of credit cards
3. living below your means
4. refraining from co-signing or giving loans
5. avoiding borrowing
6. paying cash for a car and buying a one to three years old one
7. refraining from get rich schemes
8. having only one checking account
9. tithing ten percent of your income to the church and giving offerings
10. refraining from impulse buying

Sit down together and be in unity on what to cut from your budget. Identify the *enemy* of the debt you possess, and plan a strategy for fighting and winning this battle. Fighting might involve selling items you don't need, items you're not using, or those you've stored for "a rainy day." (It's a rainy day.) Canceling subscriptions to magazines, apps. on phones and computers, or extra channels for the television may be a help. Temporarily adjusting to one car to accomplish your goal can be part of the solution. Agree and budget, budget, budget. Stand firm. Collectors and bankruptcy are not your friends.

To stay out of debt, there are certain steps that should be taken:
1. Insurance is a must – medical, home, auto, and life.
2. Have an emergency fund of three to six month's salary in case of a job loss.
3. Save for college instead of acquiring loans.
4. Set boundaries; it makes life easier when the majority of decisions are already made. Being consistent decreases stress.
5. Investing is wise; just wisely invest.
6. Invest ten to fifteen percent of your income for retirement.
7. Have a trust or a will. Don't leave your children's inheritance to the government.

A book probably could be written on each of these topics, but that will not be me writing them. However, I do want you thinking about each area, so hopefully, you'll pursue the best avenue for your lives together.

This area of finances has probably been the weakest area in the Kyle marriage. We've made poor choices, mainly in investing. Making mind (logical) decisions instead of heart (God's desire) choices have been one of our challenges to overcome. We've made great strides in accomplishing financial freedom. I'm looking forward to crossing the finish line.

One of the boundaries that Kirby and I set at the beginning of our marriage dealt with spending. If a purchase was going to cost more than twenty five dollars, we had to be in agreement before the purchase was made. That action kept us in balance and promoted unity in our spending. Also, one checking account has helped.

We have been faithful with the tithe; ten percent has been our norm. We're cheerful givers; we love to give. We see the tithe as a covering over us. It is a reminder to God to rebuke the devourer concerning our finances. About fifteen years ago, the Lord wanted us to start giving offerings above the tithe. We've been faithful to plant into good soil. Through offerings, we sow seed for producing a harvest of thirty, sixty, and one hundred fold return (Matthew 13:23). We want to be blessed, so we can be a blessing.

There are those who talk about money as a disease – the root of all evil. The truth is that the *love* of money is the root of all evil (1 Timothy 6:10). God doesn't want us serving two masters (Matthew 6:24). However, haven't you noticed that money is the avenue by which most transactions are made? It's the system that our government has set for trade and commerce. Without money, bartering or stealing is what is left.

Prosperity is a subject frequently discussed in the Bible. Being a child of the King (God Almighty) makes us wealthy because we're under the covenant God made with Abraham. We need to remember that God's the supplier of our need (Philippians 4:19). He's the one that promotes and gives upgrades. He tells us to prepare our profession before establishing a household (Proverbs 24:27). In Luke 6:47–48, Jesus talks about those coming to Him, hearing and doing what He says. He equates obedience to building a house on a rock.

He talks about bringing tithes into the church so that "...there may be meat in mine house; and prove me now herewith, saith the Lord of hosts, if I will not open you the windows of heaven, and pour you out a blessing, that there shall not be room enough to receive it" (Malachi 3:10). Besides God saying that we should tithe, that's a pretty good reason to tithe, don't you think?

Luke 6:38 talks about being a giver. "Give, and it shall be given unto you; good measure, pressed down, and shaken together, and running over, shall men give into your bosom. For with the same measure that ye mete withal it shall be measured to you again." We're to do good; we're to give to those that are in need. Be a big giver; you cannot out give God.

We're trustees of the Lord's money, and we're accountable as to how we use His money. Being wasteful is not a good idea.

For a moment, dream with me. What would you do if you didn't have bills to pay? There is so much freedom being debt free. When you're debt free, money does not rule or dictate. It's much easier to make wise choices God's way. Accepting the right job or profession instead of *more money* dictating is a prime example. Being in God's will with no debt is huge! You could truly say in general, "No worries! Be happy!"

What does our financial challenge look like?
What changes do we need to make to become debt free?

Deuteronomy 28:12b
Romans 13:8
Matthew 13:23
1 Timothy 6:10
Matthew 6:24

Philippians 4:19
Proverbs 24:27
Luke 6:47–48
Malachi 3:10
Luke 6:38

Parenting – Do We Want Children?

I'm sure there are couples who are plagued by this question. Many have had a hard upbringing and may believe that they would be horrible parents. Some just want freedom to do their own thing. "No children to hold me back" might be their motto. There are those who are unable to conceive. From the opposite perspective, some want eleven for their very own football team. Personally, I wanted to provide well for my children. The number of children depended upon that ability. Ultimately, ask God how many children you should raise. He'll tell you, and He'll tell you when to have them.

God is also a God who loves to bless. I wanted a boy first and a girl second, two years apart. I birthed Jeff first, and then twenty three months later, Lauri was born. They're such blessings in my life. God loves to give us the desires of our heart.

In Genesis, God says to be fruitful and multiply and replenish the earth. Psalm 127:5 says, "Happy is the man that hath his quiver full." When Jesus was on the earth, He wanted the little children to come to Him. He gave honor to them by giving recognition, love and peace. That pretty much dispels the old adage that children should be seen, not heard.

First, let's address being a great parent. Like with marriage, it takes becoming the *best* you can be, to be that great parent. Becoming free of past baggage is so important.

The easy part of parenting usually is the body or the outward part: food, clothing, and shelter. The more challenging part of raising a child the Lord's way is the inward part of spirit and soul. Parents have most control in the physical. However, in the spirit and soul (mind, will, and emotions), guidance is required. Hopefully, our children want to obey their parents and make wise decisions.

As parents, we need to leave anger, frustration, fear, poor self image, shame, guilt, codependency, and the like out of discipline. As a reminder, renounce lies believed, embrace the truth, and forgive to be set free. Always be teachable. "Know-it-alls" don't make it very far. Self improvement always enhances your circumstances. Maintaining the proper attitude when disciplining a child is a must. NO anger! There will be more on this subject later.

I want to title this next segment *Tips for Parenting*. I have divided these tips into eight topics:

Topic One Parents, be sure you're in agreement when you address an issue with your children. Otherwise, an argument will probably ensue, if not with children, with your mate. Having unity on a subject decreases stress and produces peace and harmony in the long run.

I believe Kirby and I have had many more confrontations on raising our children than on any other subject in our marriage. Kirby was allowed to stay out all night, if he wanted, as long as he was in bed before his parents woke up the next morning. Now for me, I grew up with a night curfew of ten thirty or eleven. You can see the chasm that had to be crossed. Dealing with curfews ahead of time before addressing the issue with our children decreased much hassle, bickering, and tempers flaring. We actually sat down and had an intelligent conversation with our children on what was expected of them, and they openly shared their thoughts.

Be on the same page. When your children find out you're not of one mind, they will play one against the other in hopes of getting their wishes met. We don't need to be teaching manipulation.

Topic Two Let's cover the roles of parents. Fathers are designed to *protect, provide, and give identity* to their children. Man was created by God first, then woman. God designed man to be over his family. Generally, man is built larger and with stronger muscles to equip him for his purpose of protection.

Society has placed pay scales higher for men than women to help with provision. Men usually receive better wages. They are very logical, focused, and job orientated. Have you ever tried to talk to a male that's absorbed with work on the computer? It's an act of congress to get his attention. (I may be exaggerating a little bit.)

I really want to address the third roll of the father – identity. There is a statistic that states father abandonment is in almost half of the family units in America today. Many fathers have produced children and shirked their responsibility of parenting. Having worked with homeless pregnant women for fifteen years, I have seen the affects left behind: codependency, fear, anger, a poor self image, control issues, and more. Identity is a vital part of a child's life. Even when Jesus was baptized by John the Baptist, Papa God acknowledged His son by saying, "Thou art my beloved Son, in whom I am well pleased" (Mark 1:11).

Speaking over our children is vital. I believe God puts in us a desire to know and understand who we are. Many are still asking the question, "Who am I?" Children need fathers who love unconditionally, encourage, support, and praise. Children need to hear that they're important to their earthly father and to their heavenly Father.

It's important that children know they're special and one of a kind. When the identity issue isn't addressed, girls search out their male peers to fill the void left by this abandonment. Codependency becomes a huge issue that often leads to pregnancy, prostitution, and even pornography. Sooo, what is your excuse? *Speak blessing over your children!* (Oops. I think I started preaching.)

Now let's focus on the mother's roles. God made women more emotional because they've been given caring roles over the children. As mothers, we're to *nurture, comfort, and teach.* We're to support and raise our children to maturity.

When I think of the word nurture, I think of nursing a baby. God physically designed women uniquely for just that function – to feed. All children should have proper nourishment, safe water to drink, adequate sleep, and appropriate exercise to remain healthy. Moms play a vital role seeing that the physical bodies of their children are clean, healthy, and at their best. This is just an automatic response to nurturing.

Let's look at comfort. Comfort comes in different forms. As a baby, comfort means, "Are my needs being met?" Having a full tummy, a clean diaper, cuddle time, and plenty of rest says comfort. As a child grows older, this word changes in meaning. Comfort looks more like, "Are you there to help me when I can't do it myself?" It takes on the look of support, approval, and love. It picks up the pieces that seem impossible to repair. It also puts the bandaids on scraped elbows and knees and shows compassion while consoling a broken heart. It might be a word of advice to a teenager who needs direction and clarity. Truth produces freedom for a receptive ear. Hugs and kisses should be the norm.

In many cases, I believe less thought is given to teaching children because of so many responsibilities of parents. However, as grandparents, we have more time to invest, and teaching becomes major. I believe the phrase, "It takes a village to raise a child" must have been coined in this situation. Scripture says, "Train up a child in the way he should go: and when he is old, he will not depart from it" (Proverbs 22:6). Even though this scripture is referencing a good name and finances, we're to train our children to be whole, to be the *best* they can be spirit, soul, and body.

Spiritually, are they learning who God is? Are they reading and studying the Word, worshiping in a church, and enjoying healthy friendships? Do they have the opportunity to know Jesus personally?

Looking at the soul, exposing a mind to good is paramount. Clean entertainment might look like family activities, movies that teach good moral values, computer games that stretch learning, outside sports, or inside games such as chess or checkers. Today, home schooling is a great way to educate children. However, if that is not an option for you, be sure your children don't miss developing their moral code, values, talents, and abilities. These teachings grow little ones up to maturity. Needless to say, your teaching is vitally important.

Topic Three Parents, be a good listener. Sometimes children can figure out the answer on their own by just talking about the issue. Many times, they don't want someone to "fix it." They just want to vent and be heard. When parents do give advice, hopefully asked for, it's really important to determine the real issue.

Usually, what appears to be the problem covers up the real issue. For instance, if a child's using drugs or drinking alcohol, the drugs or alcohol are not the problem. That's their escape route. There may be some form of abuse that is the real issue. If a child's lashing out and cussing in anger, most likely the anger isn't from the immediate situation but from past situations that haven't been resolved. I'm reminded often when working with single moms that hurting people hurt people. We only give away what we have.

This example comes from a six year old little girl who, being one of the youngest in her class, was asked to read out loud in front of her classmates. When mispronouncing a word, everyone broke out in laughter, including the teacher. The laughter was not curtailed. Therefore, the judgments that she took on were humiliation, rejection, and helplessness, to name a few. She believed everyone was against her, and no one would ever listen to her. After all, she *is* stupid. She became shy and believed she was not important and would never be important in this world. She was a failure – a nobody. Fear became the controlling factor in her life. Everything was filtered through fear. This incident was a crushing blow to a little mercy girl whose personality is to do things right, be dependable and organized. Crying nightly over homework seemed to be the issue, when in truth, it was over the event in class and what she believed of herself. Yes, that little mercy girl was me.

It is important to question your child and make sure the interpretation of a situation is correct. Children tend to take everything to heart. Lies we believe become facts about ourselves – truths. "They don't like me. I should have done___. I, I, I." Satan wants us to believe lies. That's one of his greatest tools to steal, kill, and destroy our witness. Be a good listener when interacting with your children. Use eye to eye contact. Give them your undivided attention: be relatable, be positive, be uplifting, and have empathy. At least look pleasant. A smile would be nice, if appropriate.

Always explain *why*. Sometimes it saves a lot of heartache on both parties. If I'd known that my early curfew all through high school was intended for my protection, I would not have believed the lie that "My parents don't trust me." This lie was believed for over ten years.

Remember, we're not perfect human beings. We make mistakes. One of my favorite was blaming my children for something they didn't do. When we make mistakes, be sure to apologize and ask for forgiveness. Otherwise, you'll be seen as a mean, lying, and unfair person. Making amends brings peace and mends the relationship. It's a wonderful thing!

Topic Four Observe your child. Discover your little one's love language. This can make a huge difference in how your child perceives a parent's love. To refresh your memory, these are your choices:
1. undivided attention
2. gifts
3. acts of service
4. affirmation
5. physical touch

Topic Five Knowing your child's personality is also a plus. To refresh your memory, they are as follows:
1. sanguine, a "social butterfly"
2. choleric, the leader or boss
3. melancholy, the organized and dependable one
4. phlegmatic, the layed back and easy going one

For the sanguine, having a large number of siblings and a plethora of friends would look like a bit of heaven. Cholerics need something or someone to lead. My granddaughter, Mercy, is primarily choleric. Giving Mercy the job of bossing the dog around when she was little, solved many issues between siblings and parents.

Most likely, if you need a job finished to perfection, get your melancholy child to help. Learn how to motivate your phlegmatic one. Find what works for you in your family and in your circumstances.

Accept each child for who they are and how they are made. Develop their bent. Observe your little individual. Does he have an interest in science, computers, or architecture? Does she like music or art? Is your child a born leader or a server? In the future, would he function best being self employed or working for a company? Help develop strengths and overcome weaknesses in your little one.

Topic Six It's important to dedicate your child to the Lord. This is probably the first step in raising a child in the admonition of the Lord. Then introduce your little one to Jesus. No one knows when that opportunity will occur. Just be alert and seize the moment.

Every year, Kirby and I have the privilege of having Aaron spend a week with his Nana B and Papa K. Last year, as we were driving to pick up a friend, seven year old Aaron asks me if it's Christian music playing on the radio. I reply, "Yes. Do you like it?" Aaron replied that he did. Then after a long pause, he states matter of factly, "I want to know Jesus." I had not expected that statement. I was just driving along, singing and thinking about the friend we were about to pick up. I said, "Well, okay." I told him to repeat after me; we prayed. Then I asked, "So Aaron, do you know, that you know, that you know Jesus?" His reply was, "Yes, and I will never change my mind." WOW! What a moment – an everlasting moment.

Don't miss yours. Just like you, your children need a foundation. Teach them how to hear from God so they will know their purpose and direction in life. Having peace about the right calling, being in the right place in life, brings great satisfaction.

Topic Seven Let's look at discipline. Not long ago, I listened to a DVD by Thomas W. Phelan, Ph.D. called *More 1-2-3 Magic*[8]. I learned some great advice for moms and dads. To give you an overview, five areas were pinpointed as times when children might need discipline: getting dressed and out of the house in the morning, eating at meal time, getting homework, picking up toys or cleaning their room, and going to bed at the appointed time. Looking back over the years of raising my children, I whole heartedly agreed with him.

Dr. Phelan shared ways to deal with these stressful times. I learned eight ways to encourage good behavior:
1. Praise your child and use positive reinforcement. Speak blessings over them. (It takes four positive moments to override one negative one.)
2. Make corrections in a loving manner. Yet, be firm and simple. No dissertations are needed here. Using a compliment or praise before and after a correction may help your child accept the correction better.
3. A kitchen timer can be a great device for dealing with homework assignments and time outs. Mechanical objects cannot be manipulated.
4. The docking system also can be an effective tool. When we, as parents, end up doing the chores designated for our children, the children pay their parents the wages due them from their piggy bank.

5. Let natural consequences have the proper effect. An example might be allowing your child to be late for school which puts the situation in the hands of the principal. There's no rescuing here.
6. Let's discuss charts. A chart would show duties or chores that need to be done by a certain time. Be sure rewards are given for a job well done. (That is their pay.) Be sure that the assigned jobs are age appropriate.
7. You can always count to three.
8. Before leaving the house, explain what is expected of your children.

Before I'd go to the grocery store with my two preschoolers, I would let them know, "You can choose only *one* item to bring home from the store. If you whine about wanting more, you will not get to buy anything." The explanation was simple and direct. Both would go back and forth the whole grocery experience trying to figure out what one item they each wanted to purchase. Boundaries are important. Letting my children know what to expect ahead of time, eliminated bickering and complaining. Peace reigned, and that's what we want. Right?

Proverbs 13:24 tells us to discipline our children, even if it requires spanking. This proverb instructs the parent not about spanking alone but about a loving parent who disciplines. Discipline sets boundaries. It lets our children know what is important and that they are loved.

Please remember that you're not alone in parenting. Pray! The Lord can show you ways to get your strong willed one reined back in. It is paramount to refrain from anger when disciplining. Walk away from the situation temporarily, take deep breaths, or count to ten. Whatever works for you, learn to *act*, not react.

I wish I could say this was the norm for me in raising my children. Too many times I resorted to yelling at them or using the *you* word too much, attacking character. I remember one day when Jeff was about four years old, it seemed we were constantly on each other's nerves. After quite a few reprimands in a short period of time, Jeff decided to run away from home. He went so far as to pack up his little red wagon and start making it up the stairs and out the door. I calmly said, "If you leave now, you are going to miss Grandmother and Granddaddy that are coming for Christmas." Jeff decided to stay until they left. While this is a bit comical, it made me stop and think about how I was acting and sounding. I needed to choose grace and love more. Learn from your mistakes. Saying you are wrong goes a long way to advance healing in a relationship. God restores.

When disciplining older children, knowing the correct direction to turn a child around without leaving bitterness and resentment is crucial. Showing honor and respect to your children is a key element. This shows your children that they're important and valuable. Consequences may be in the form of having cell phone usage cut, limiting computer games and television, taking the car keys, or grounding. These usually work. What works for one does not mean it will work for the other. Hopefully your child is smart and will learn from experiences of others, instead of having to deal with his own consequences. Hopefully, because you honor him, he'll honor you.

I'm taking bragging rights at this moment. I've been superbly impressed with my son's and daughter-in-law's parenting skills. They have four children: Mercy, Alyssa, Jordan, and Ethan. Over the past ten years, I've taken all four on outings almost every other Friday. Because they are well behaved, I can take these four children anywhere. The most impressive technique I have seen Jeff and Amy use is showing respect and honoring their children. These two discipline in love and in private. These four children are not embarrassed or put down in front of others. The issue is addressed immediately and directly. Their character is not verbally attacked with, "How stupid can you be?" or "How could you?" My grandchildren have positive self images because their parents address the issue instead of attacking character. Growing their children God's way is a priority.

It's very important for children to know that consequences follow disobedience. It's also imperative that there be consistency with discipline. Otherwise, children will not believe you when you speak. Their belief system will say, "I'll get away with it."

It's very important not to take on the belief that your child's actions are always a reflection upon you as a parent. This concept took me a number of years of much correction (nagging) from this perfectionist person to discover that I don't control my children's lives. They, too, have a mind of their own to make choices just like I do. They're responsible for their actions. As parents, we're only responsible for our actions. I had to stop labeling myself as a terrible parent when my children misbehaved.

I think my favorite saying pertaining to making wise choices is "Two wrongs don't make a right." In other words, getting back at someone inappropriately because he hurt you or marrying someone just because you're pregnant, doesn't turn the situation around for good. Does this sound familiar? Make God choices.

Our goal is to lovingly set boundaries to build character in our children's lives for the future. It's important to have adults in adulthood. They should become responsible loving individuals that take ownership and demonstrate leadership. Because they're teachable, they should be growing. They're free of past baggage, wise, and trustworthy. Their faith is grounded in Papa God, Jesus, and the Holy Spirit. *Welcome to parenting!*

Topic Eight I want to speak directly to teaching children. As parents, we need to be sure we're teaching our children on a level they can understand. If we're talking over their heads, our words are futile. Repeating back to parents what was heard is important. It's amazing how interpretation can be skewed or totally wrong. Possibly, your words just were not heard. Teaching is repetitive. If your child does not get *it* the first time, persevere; don't give up. Keeping communication open is vitally important.

Teach your children subject matter that is age appropriate. You want them to listen. Find material that interests them. My children love animals, so I found *Purpose Life*[9] journals that used different animals to teach object lessons and principles of importance. We looked at God's power in us through the oxen, humility through the peacock, leadership through the giraffe, wisdom through the eagle, and others. Reading regularly is a must. Find materials where your children can participate.

Bedtime always appeared to be the best reading time for us. I seemed to have their undivided attention. Using Bible stories, I would teach them about Jesus and how to become more like Him. Knowing fully the Trinity (Father, Son, and Holy Spirit) and seeing what God says about them are huge in the ability to build faith. Our children need to know their identity.

As Jeff and Lauri grew older, we went to the library frequently to check out books that caught their interest. During the summer, it was common for each child to check out five books for the week. Be creative.

Use events of the day to teach. Many specimens of nature are great teachers. Choose from a plethora of rocks, bugs, flowers, trees, and birds. Check out the pond at the park. Climbing trees, constructing forts, and building camp fires teach as well as bring family unity. Household duties are a teaching ground for responsibility. If conflict arises, deal with it promptly. If improper speech is used, correct it. If laziness or procrastination has crept in, motivate. If a lie is being spoken, counteract it with truth.

As parents, we need to live out what we teach, or it will not be accepted. Much of what children learn is what they see at home. Be a great example.

A large number of excuses can be made for why we don't spend the time required to develop strong, mature, God-fearing adults. However, when parents see that they set precedence on how grandchildren and great grandchildren could be raised, good teaching can be seen as a need and set as a priority. Much of how we're raised gets handed down. We affect generations.

It's important to remember that regardless of the circumstances in which we were raised, good choices still can be made. Don't make excuses. It's about finishing our race well.

I want my children and grandchildren to remember the good, to pass down a worthy legacy – an inheritance – one that honors the Lord. I hope you do too.

Should we have children?
Is parenting for me?

Psalm 37:4   Proverbs 22:6
Genesis 1:28   Mark 1:11
Psalm 127:5   Proverbs 13:24
Mark 10:14

How Do I Deal with Loss?

In our life time, it would be naive for us to believe that we're immune to loss. I know I've hoped that I could only experience good in life. Unfortunately, loss happens. Loss comes in many forms: loss of a friend, divorce, bodily injury, moving, children leaving home, bankruptcy, or the death of someone close. These can be devastating to us, and depending upon how we perceive them, we can be deeply affected. It may manifest in our spirit, soul and/or body. We grieve.

We can become bitter or better through losses. It's our choice. Do we want to grow and become more mature in life, be closer to our Lord, be stronger, and be better at helping others? Or does wallowing in self pity (woe is me), being bitter, depressed, and miserable suit us better? People deal with loss differently and at different rates. A person can withdraw, and even productivity at work can be affected. We can blame others and even ourselves. The processing of loss can be quick; for others, it's not so fast.

If this area of loss is where you're stuck, I would encourage you to find a support group or a Christian counselor who's been in your shoes, who will listen to you about your wounding, and will walk beside you giving wise counsel through it. Good friends and understanding family members are also an option.

If you are a friend, please don't ignore or avoid someone whom you know is in a crisis situation. It's okay to have concern and ask, "How are you doing?" However, I want to caution you, "Don't try to fix the situation by giving unwanted advice." For the moment, having a listening ear and just being present is far more important. Sometimes all that is needed is just a big ole hug.

There are also good books out there that address loss. One of the best that I have found is titled *Good Grief*° by Granger E. Westberg. Also get into God's Word and see how our Lord sees loss. What does God say about grief? Remember, where there's a problem to overcome, there's a promise to stand on. Find that Scripture in the Bible and stand believing. We do not want to be victims; we are victors! I know one important thought that rings in my ear. What Satan means for harm, God turns to good. God restores. Stand! Let the stress from your loss bring growth.

Being a nurse, I know that medications are also used as an option for dealing with issues. However, they should be used temporarily if at all. Instead of a help, they can become a crutch to hide behind, a way of escape, and even an addiction. Medications should be used only for taking the edge off so that resolution can occur.

In living life, you realize there are different levels of grief, mainly because individuals view losses differently. The loss of a home for a single person may not be viewed as seriously as someone who is married with a family. You may have the attitude that loosing a job is no big deal; you can find another one. However, if you're a handicapped person or over sixty five years of age, loosing a job can be devastating. How you see the empty nest syndrome depends upon where you've placed your priorities in your marriage, with husband or children. A person's belief system definitely plays a roll in how one sees loss and how one reacts to it. Scripture says that Jesus wept, and yet many men grow up believing that "Big boys don't cry."

Many times we think that emotions are a sign of weakness. Let me say right here that emotions are okay. They follow our attitudes as we work through the grieving process. I'll say, it's important to give up the *why*. We could speculate that we didn't speak positive words over the situation; we doubted. We didn't fight. We had fear or anger that contributed, or we were not at the right place at the right time. Speculation can go on and on. We may never know the answer to that question while here on earth. We need to move forward by keeping our focus on *trusting God* in all things, having *hope* for the future, and showing *love* to those around us. Remember to love the Lord with all your heart, soul and mind, and love your neighbor as yourself. That's God, self, and others. Faith! Hope! Love!

The most devastating loss that's made a lasting impression on my life was the death of my third granddaughter, Naomi. Family always has been a high priority on my list, so when Naomi was stillborn, it didn't go well for me. When the nurse first said she couldn't hear a heartbeat, my first thought was, "She's new at this; the sonogram will prove her wrong." It didn't. Denial seemed to work for a moment; then reality set in. I hardly could speak through the tears as I called friends and relatives to let them know about the tragedy. You see, Naomi had been given a clean bill of health three days earlier. Naomi was just fine. There were no problems.

Naomi was delivered on Labor Day. Even though our daughter, Lauri, had delivered her at full term, she was not recognized or even given a birth date – only a death certificate. There was no recognition of life, even though she was only a week early. The doctor said she'd been dead for two days prior to delivery. We weren't able to take good presentable pictures, because her skin was so fragile.

Being a holiday, there was no one in the hospital to counsel or recommend funeral homes to view. I'll never forget leaving the hospital the next day, searching for a burial plot. It was a dreary cold day with intermittent rain. We spent most of the day driving around with a roller coaster of emotions going from one location to another having no clue who had burial plots for children or the cost. My expectations of leaving the hospital were buying outfits and anything else required for the nursery and lovingly holding our precious new little one.

Just because we had a funeral service and buried Naomi, it didn't mean all was laid to rest. We carry our experiences with us in life. How we choose to process a loss determines the outcome.

I wish I could say that after the funeral all was well. It wasn't. When I would see infants at church, it was a reminder of what I was missing. Baby showers were "a no no." I remember the drive through at Starbucks one day. The waitress was going on and on about choices when all I wanted was coffee. I hate to say this, but I was really annoyed and was ugly to her. I was angry at the world.

I went through depression for about two years, crying most every day over this loss. Lauri and I would talk often. I was privileged to talk with a counselor friend once, who gave me some fresh insight on this incident. However, I just couldn't shake the grief.

I found myself questioning. What could I have done better: prayed differently or more, been more observant (I am a nurse, you know), or been more supportive? Is serving God too hard? Hey, I have my salvation; I'm going to heaven. Is it too high a price to pay to live for the Lord? I could just do my own thing and forget serving Him. *I was angry.* It took me about four months of hashing these and other thoughts and questions to resolve most of them. My crying had slowed, but I still was depressed. For sure, I wasn't on the other side of this.

After two years, I visited my good friend in Kansas City. I figured she could be a good listening ear as well as being a wise person with sound advice. Diane and I had a great time together, enjoying each other's company and just having some fun. We ended up at the Precious Moments campus of Sam Butcher. This is such a marvelous place. Mr. Butcher has a mural of heaven that covers the entire front wall of their church. Every year, he adds another special individual that has gone on to be with the Lord. As I observed this masterpiece, I saw a small sign in the lower right hand corner that read, "No more tears." I had an inner knowing that the Lord was saying just that. Until then, I didn't know I could make choices concerning emotions. I cannot say that I haven't cried since reading that sign, but probably you could count them on one hand. I made a choice that day to choose correctly.

To recap, I was shocked and in denial. I was depressed and sobbed almost daily. I went through the *what ifs* and felt a bit guilty that I hadn't done more. I went through the anger of God allowing such a thing to happen. "She didn't get a chance to live her life here on earth to serve You and be a blessing to others." It took some time for me to resolve all that had happened and deal with all of the questions. It was a process.

Since my visit to Kansas City, I have seen fruit come from the loss of Naomi:
1. I believe Lauri and I have a closer bond than before because of walking through this loss together.
2. I have a much deeper walk with the Lord than I've ever had. I'm not just a servant. He calls me *friend*.
3. I've been able to empathize with those who have miscarried, aborted, or placed a child for adoption.

Whether it's just listening, giving a hug, or talking over the matters of the heart, I understand.

4. The Lord has allowed me to share Naomi in books. As you can see, even though her presence is in heaven, she is still making a difference on earth.
5. I bring glory and honor to my Lord because I've made it to the other side of my loss.

Our daughter, Lauri, and her husband, John have had more than their share of losses during their married lives. Having had to declare bankruptcy which in turn caused them to loose their amazing home seems like more than enough hardship. Yet, Naomi was stillborn, and their next son, Aaron, is considered a million dollar child, due to eleven blood transfusions (six inutero and five after birth), seven surgeries by the age of three, speech therapy, and on going hearing aids. I'm not even going into the job losses they have endured. (Both honor our Lord. They are well educated and are productive adults in society.)

In this past year, our son, Jeff and his wife, Amy, have had three family members with broken bones due to accidents: a farming injury, a car accident, and a fall from a trailer. Of those, two required surgery, and all three were hospitalized.

How are you going to see your losses? Are your trials always going to look like losses, something that you will never get over? Or, will you work through the loss, learn from it, and become a better person due to the circumstance? Because we live in a sinful world, we all face losses, and it's not always easy to get through them. However, I will say, "It's worth it."

Never under estimate what God can do in your circumstances. When we give Him permission to change things, He will. He has the Almighty power to do just that. You may be like Jesus saying, "My God, My God, why hast thou forsaken me"

(Matthew 27:46)? God hasn't. Jesus says, "I will never leave thee, nor forsake thee" (Hebrews 13:5). Our Lord turns things around. He wants you to taste and see that He is good. James 1:2 says that we are to count it all joy when troubles come our way. Trials produce endurance. I don't know about you, but I want to finish my purpose in life. I would like to think that my *best* would be enough for Papa God to say that I am His beloved daughter in whom He is well pleased.

**Have you gotten to the other side of your loss?
Are you rejoicing yet?**

Romans 8:28   Psalm 34:8
Matthew 27:46   James 1:2
Hebrews 13:5

What Does the *Best* Marriage Look Like?

As you can tell, I am a list maker. Therefore, I thought I might recap what we've been studying – the *best* marriage:

1. joining a man and woman by covenant
2. finding the right mate God intends you to have
3. being the *best* you can be (spirit, soul, and body)
4. loving appropriately (agape, phileo, and eros)
5. having a great marriage foundation
   - being a Christian
   - standing on covenant
   - leaving father and mother – cleaving
   - loving spouse
   - trusting spouse
6. accepting each other as we are
7. learning to communicate
8. dealing with conflict quickly and learning to forgive
9. fulfilling visions through goal setting
10. being a servant
11. taking responsibility with finances
12. being a tither and a giver of offerings
13. taking responsibility for raising our children in the way they should go
    - dads providing, protecting, and giving identity
    - moms nurturing, comforting, and teaching
14. dealing with loss God's way

As many years as I have studied Proverbs 31, never once have I heard any teaching on the virtuous male. The virtuous woman always was the featured topic.

King Lemuel was ruler over Massa during the reign of King Solomon about 960 B.C. Let's hear from King Lemuel as he expounds on his mother's teaching.

King Lemuel has much to say about men:
1. Don't waste strength on women or the ways that destroy kings.
2. It's not for kings to drink wine or strong drink, lest they forget the law and pervert judgment on any of the afflicted.
3. Speak up for those who are headed for destruction.
4. Judge righteously and plead the cause of the poor and needy.
5. Trust your wife.
6. Be well known in the city.
7. Sit among the elders of the land.
8. Honor, bless, and praise your wife.

That speaks of this young man staying out of trouble and taking responsibility and commitment seriously. This says to me that he's faithful to his wife and trusts her. He doesn't belittle her; he lifts her up. He believes in community. He not only sits with the elders and is well known, he treats people fairly. He helps the poor, the needy, and those headed for destruction. Wow! He sounds pretty amazing to me.

You may be saying, but I am not a king. Well, if you're a Christian, you're a child of the King, which makes you a prince – royalty. I would say you qualify.

Let's see what our king has to say about a virtuous woman:
1. She's one that is precious and priceless above rubies.
2. She's good to her husband all the days of her life.
3. She works willingly with her hands.
4. She wakes up while it is still night.
5. She brings food from afar and prepares meat for her household and maidens.
6. She buys a field and plants a vineyard.
7. She carries strength.
8. She perceives that her merchandise is good; she does what it takes to make it so.
9. She continues to work into the night.
10. She works with her hands making thread and producing fabric.
11. She gives to the poor and needy.
12. She's not afraid of the snow (death), because her household is clothed with warm clothes of scarlet.
13. She makes coverings of tapestry
14. She clothes herself with silk and purple.
15. She makes fine linen garments and sashes and sells them to merchants.
16. She portrays strength and honor and is not concerned for the future.
17. She speaks wisely and is kind.
18. She watches over her household and is not lazy.
19. Her children honor her and bless her.
20. She fears the Lord.
21. The fruit of her hands declare her praise in the gates.

To sum up this precious gem, the virtuous woman is one that is good to her husband. She's not lazy. She rises early to purchase and prepare food for her household and stays up late making fabric to sew warm clothing and tapestry for cold weather. She's wise, kind, strong, and a good business woman (buying a field and selling merchandise). Her children think well of her. She holds the Lord in awe and is praised and honored because of her fruitfulness.

Both of these renditions say much as to how a husband and wife should present themselves in marriage: strong, solid, and healthy. We are to reign as King and Queen.

On a scale of 1–10, how would you rate your marriage? Do you see your marriage growing into God's *best*?

Proverbs 31:1–31

Is There a Time when
We Have Arrived?

I would love to tell you that some day you can exclaim, "I made it. No more sin is in my life. I am perfect!" Not. We were born with a sinful nature. There's never a time when we have it all together. We still make choices, and poor ones seem to happen among the wise ones. As a Christian, our spirit has arrived. We are the righteousness of God through Christ Jesus. I believe the more right choices we make, the closer we are to *arriving* in soul and body. Renewing our minds in the Word to choose good in each decision process does take us closer to our goal. The ultimate is to be like Jesus in spirit, soul, and body. I wish I could say we could always think pure thoughts, make perfect choices, and have the proper emotions. Even the great missionary, Paul, said that he would decide to choose one way but would do another. However, I don't believe we should wallow in self pity and give up. I look at this earth as a training ground for heaven.

Striving to move on to higher planes and experiencing upgrades are important. Living our lives knowing that we have been placed on earth for our purpose – a purpose that is just ours and no one else's – and having direction to accomplish it, is pretty amazing.

I don't know about you, but I want my purpose to be the *best* purpose it can be:

1. I want my profession as nurse, wife, mother, grandmother, lay counselor, and author to be the *best*.
2. I want my relationship with those around me to be blessed.
3. I want my relationship with my heavenly Father, Jesus, and the Holy Spirit to be amazing.

I truly believe our *best* is all that is required of any of us as we stay in Him. God made forgiveness for those times when our *best* is less. Forgiveness sets us free so we can get back on the right path to being our *best* again.

This all holds true in marriage as well. Marriage is also a growing process. I will say that the longer Kirby and I have been married, the fewer conflicts we encounter. That doesn't mean we always agree, but we have the tools to defuse our differences. We strive to stay in unity.

Over the years, we get to know our spouse better. We learn more and better ways to serve our mate, and we cherish each other more deeply. Life is sweeter. (Remember rewards are at the end of the race.)

There are truly seasons in our lives, and they can all be great! How we see life matters. Is the glass half empty, or is the glass half full? Usually *change* comes with seasons, and many people resist change. Again, are we looking at change as an opportunity for growth or something to escape? Just like spring, summer, autumn, and winter, we also have seasons in our lives.

Mine have looked like childhood, grade school, school of nursing, career, marriage, children, grandchildren, self-employment, and retirement. I could add others like moving, health issues, relationships, diet and job changes. I'm sure the list has not been exhausted.

The Bible speaks about seasons in Ecclesiastes 3:1–8. "To every thing there is a season, and a time to every purpose under the heaven." These are the times:

1. to be born and to die
2. to plant and to pluck up what is planted
3. to kill and to heal
4. to break down and to build up
5. to weep and to laugh
6. to mourn and to dance
7. to cast away stones and to gather stones together
8. to embrace and to refrain from embracing
9. to get and to lose
10. to keep and to cast away
11. to rend and to sew
12. to keep silent and to speak
13. to love and to hate
14. of war and of peace

I believe when we've completed our final season, we'll be able to proclaim together, "Heaven! What a glorious day!". Ultimately, when we all see Jesus, we'll sing and shout the victory. So, count it all joy!

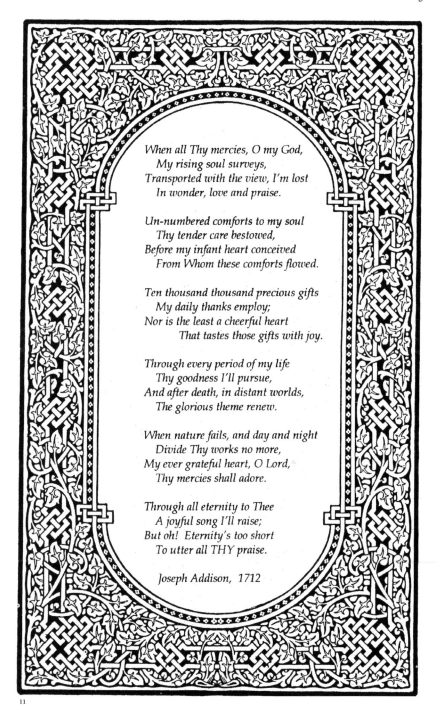

When all Thy mercies, O my God,
   My rising soul surveys,
Transported with the view, I'm lost
   In wonder, love and praise.

Un-numbered comforts to my soul
   Thy tender care bestowed,
Before my infant heart conceived
   From Whom these comforts flowed.

Ten thousand thousand precious gifts
   My daily thanks employ;
Nor is the least a cheerful heart
      That tastes those gifts with joy.

Through every period of my life
   Thy goodness I'll pursue,
And after death, in distant worlds,
   The glorious theme renew.

When nature fails, and day and night
   Divide Thy works no more,
My ever grateful heart, O Lord,
   Thy mercies shall adore.

Through all eternity to Thee
   A joyful song I'll raise;
But oh! Eternity's too short
   To utter all THY praise.

   Joseph Addison, 1712

11

Another Season!

What new season are you entering?
How do you perceive it?

2 Corinthians 5:21   Ecclesiastes 3:1–8
Romans 7:19   Romans 7:19

Notes

1   Banning Liebscher, *Rooted*, (Colorado: WaterBrook Press, 2016).

2   Florence Littauer, *Personality Plus*, (Michigan: Fleming H. Revell, 1992).

3   Don Colbert, M.D., *Let Food Be Your Medicine*, (Tennessee: Worthy Books, 2016).

4   Gary Chapman, *The Five Love Languages*, (Illinois: Northfield Publishing, 2015).

5   Dr. David and Teresa Ferguson, *Intimate Encounters*, (Texas: Intimacy Press, 1997).

6   Ibid.

7   Dave Ramsey, *The Total Money Makeover*, (Tennessee: Thomas Nelson, Inc., 2003).

8   Thomas Phelan, Ph.D., DVD, *More 1-2-3 Magic*, (Illinois: ParentMagic Inc., 2004).

9   Institute in Basic Life Principles, *Purpose Life*, (Illinois: Institute in Basic Life Principles).

10 Granger E. Westberg, *Good Grief*, (Minnesota: Augsburg Fortress, 1997).

11 Joseph Addison, an untitled poem of gratitude and praise, (public domain, 1712).

Acknowledgements

Even though books should be inspired works of God, much goes on behind the scenes to accomplish such a work. I have such appreciation and gratitude for these amazing people in my life.

To my husband, Kirby Kyle, my lover and best friend, not only have you been my sounding board, you've been my computer whiz. I cannot thank you enough for putting up with all I am *not* in the computer world. I love you always.

To my son and daughter-in-law, Jeff and Amy Kyle, thank you for being a great role model for bringing up children in the way they should go. What a blessing you are in my life. Hugs!

To my daughter and son-in-law, Lauri and John Berka, thank you for being over comers, standing through it all. Lauri, your artistic abilities amaze me. Even when I've been indecisive, you've been gracious. I so appreciate all your hard work. Hugs!

To my grandchildren – Mercy, Alyssa, Jordan, Ethan, Joshua, Aaron, and Naomi – you've been my inspiration for writing. What a blessing you are to me. Pass on to the next generation what you've learned. I love you lots.

To my dear friend, Jana Greer, thank you for all your time and expertise editing this work to make it the best. You are cherished.

To my special friend, Linda Vettes, whom God sent to walk beside me, you've been a huge supporter and encourager. Your editing and marketing skills are so appreciated. Thank you from the bottom of my heart.

To my dear friends Kay Bennett and Diane O'Neal, you've blessed my life more than you know. You are precious in my sight.

Other Books by Glenda Kyle

Children's Christmas Activities is a compilation of skits, activities, and plays that will make your Christmas the holiday of the year.

These are the benefits that you will realize:
1. Children grow in creativity, self-esteem, and knowledge of the Lord.
2. Family unity is nurtured.
3. You invest in future generations.
4. You share Jesus with others.
5. Jesus is honored – given first place – during His birthday celebration.

Come and see.

My Child, Walk With Me is an autobiography of Kyle's life from age six onward. She relates the poor and wise choices made in her relationship with the Lord. "I want others to know how special it is to be in God's presence, to hear Him speak, to know truth, and be set free. God, who is all knowing, omnipresent, most powerful, and Creator of all, wants to walk and talk with you because He loves you so much. Walking with God is exciting; He's not boring. Walking with Him is only a choice away."

A soulfully enriching testament of divine love abounds with profound spiritual messages for everyone.

Printed in the United States
By Bookmasters